The Crest-Jewel of Wisdom

and other writings of

Śankarâchârya

Translations and Commentaries by
CHARLES JOHNSTON

Theosophical University Press
Covina, California

THEOSOPHICAL UNIVERSITY PRESS
COVINA, CALIFORNIA

First Edition, 1946

PRINTED IN THE UNITED STATES OF AMERICA

Preface

THIS little volume with its foundation-stones of Truth is an effort to further the second object of the Theosophical Society as it was originally expressed by H. P. Blavatsky in *The Key to Theosophy:*

To promote the study of Aryan and other Scriptures, of the World's religion and sciences, and to vindicate the importance of old Asiatic literature, namely, of the Brahmanical, Buddhist, and Zoroastrian philosophies.

The translations herein are reprints from the *Oriental Department Papers* published by William Quan Judge in 1894, 1895, and 1896, as well as from Judge's Magazine, *The Path.* In introducing Charles Johnston, then a member of the Theosophical Society, as the translator of the Sanskrit works to be produced in his Oriental Papers, Judge writes:

Of his qualifications there is no doubt, as he has had experience in this field, has also for some time been teaching Sanskrit, and brings to the work a sincere sympathy with Indian thought as well as devotion to the Society which will without question make the matter furnished of value as well as of interest.

In Śankârâchârya (the blessed teacher) we have an example of the statement that "Masters are living facts." Mankind needs such assurance these days, and needs not only the inspiration of the story of a man who has lived divinely, but also his kindly and strengthening words of wisdom. What greater gift could the Hindu sage have left us than that of a collection of soul-stirring thoughts?

For those who, with hearts fervent with compassion, seek

the holy path that brings to birth a 'sage of boundless vision,' Śankarâchârya's *Crest-Jewel of Wisdom* will be a practical and inspiring guide to life. Its teachings, the shared realizations of an enlightened god-man, tell us the laws by which we may 'untie the bonds of unwisdom,' and thus, evermore free, with minds calm and pellucid and hearts purified of reward-desiring actions, come to know and partake of the majestic power, light, and universal kinship of the Divine within us, our birthright as humans, and our passport to grander attainments in vaster spheres of consciousness.

Just as the sun with its splendor and its glories greets us every morning when we awake and silently through the day nourishes us in all parts of our being, and later as it sets at night, leaves a glow of rich color suggesting a spiritual mystery to be grasped somewhere, somehow — maybe in the morn's returning light — so the challenging message of Śankarâchârya's jewel-thoughts braces the spirits of world-weary ones as they turn to its radiant wisdom. They become illumined by the divine fire permeating its words, and as they turn from the study of its verses enriched for another of life's experiences, the glow of the gleaned awakenings will become a haunting memory leading them back to its precepts for another sunrise and sunset of the spirit.

JUDITH TYBERG

Theosophical University
March, 1946

Table of Contents

Introductory

BY CHARLES JOHNSTON

Śankara, the Teacher

THE Upanishads, Buddha, and Śankara: these are the three great lights of Indian wisdom. The Upanishads far away in the golden age; in the bright dawn that has faded so many ages ago. Buddha, the Awakened One, who, catching in his clear spirit the glow of that early dawn, sought to reflect it in the hearts of all men, of whatever race, of whatever nation; sought to break down the barriers of caste and priestly privilege; to leave each man alone with the Universe, with no mediator between. But scattering abroad the rays of wisdom, Buddha found that the genius of each man, of each race, could only reflect one little beam; and that in thus making the light the property of all men, the purity and completeness of the light might be impaired.

Then followed Śankarâchârya — Śankara the Teacher — who set himself to the preservation of the light; to burnishing the casket that held the lamp of wisdom. Busying himself chiefly with India, he saw that the light must be preserved, as far as its completeness and perfection were concerned, within the Brahman order, where the advantages of heredity, of ages of high ideals and rigid discipline could best secure the purity of the light; could best supply a body of men, fitted by character and training to master the high knowledge, to sustain the moral effort that made the glory of India's Golden Age.

This task of fitting the Brahman order to carry the torch of wisdom was undertaken by Śankara the Teacher in three ways. First, by commenting on the Great Upanishads and the Bhagavad Gîtâ, he rendered the knowledge of the Golden Age into the thought and language of the Brahmans of his day. Second, by writing a series of preparatory works, of catechisms and manuals, he made smooth the path of those who would take the first steps on the path of wisdom. Thirdly, by a system of reform and discipline within the Brahman order, he did all that sound practice could do to second clear precept.

The system formed by Śankara within the Brahman order largely continues at the present day. The radiant points of this system are the monasteries founded by the Teacher, where a succession of teachers, each initiated by his predecessor, carry on the spiritual tradition of the great Śankara unbroken.

Of commentaries on the Upanishads and the Bhagavad Gîtâ, many, perhaps, were written in a gradual series leading up from the simple truths to the more profound mysteries; so that, with one after another of these treatises in hand, the learner was gradually led to the heart of the mystery which lies "like a germ of generation" well concealed in these matchless theosophic documents. These commentaries were followed by others, the work of Śankara's pupils; and though these works of explanation are very numerous, all those that are published seem to belong to the earlier stages of learning, and leave the deeper passages and problems of the Upanishads still unsolved.

But the other part of Śankara's work, the manuals and catechisms for learners, are complete and perfect. They really teach, quite plainly and lucidly, the first steps on the path of wisdom; they point out, with clear insistence, the qualities that are necessary to make these first steps fruitful; qualities without which the learner may remain, hesitating and halting, on the threshold, through lack of the force and sterling moral worth which alone make any further progress possible.

Nor are these necessary qualities difficult to understand. They are not queer psychic powers that only flatter vanity; they are not mere intellectual tricks that leave the heart cold; they are rather the simple qualities of sterling honesty, of freedom from selfishness and sensuality — which have formed the basis of every moral code; the virtues so common and commonplace on the lips, but not quite so common in the life and character.

These treatises of Śankara speak to the common understanding and moral sense in an unparalleled degree. They are an appeal to the reason that has hardly ever been equalled for clearness and simplicity by the sages of the earth. Their aim is Freedom (Moksha), "Freedom from the bondage of the world." This aim speaks to every one, awakens an echo in every heart, appeals to the universal hope of common humanity.

But it is not enough for the mind to follow the lucid sentences of Śankara. "Freedom from the bondage of the world" demands something more. "Sickness is not cured by saying 'Medicine,' but by drinking it; so a man is not set free by the name of the Eternal, but by

discerning the Eternal." The teaching must be woven
into life and character if it is to bear fruit; it is not
enough to contemplate the virtue of freedom from
selfishness and sensuality in the abstract.

One of these treatises, "The Crest-Jewel of Wisdom,"
will be translated here. It will be divided according
to the natural sections of the text, beginning with the
first steps on the path and ending with the complete
teaching of Śankara's philosophy so far as that teaching
can be put into words. Hardly any notes will be necessary, as the language of the teacher is lucidity itself.
Every word is defined and every definition enlarged
and repeated.

It is not, however, the object of these papers to put
forward a presentation of eastern thought merely to be
read and forgotten. We shall spare no pains of repeti-
tion and amplification to make the thoughts of the
East quite clear. But much remains to be done by
readers themselves. They must make the thoughts of
Śankara and the sages their own spiritual property if
they are to benefit by them, and as a preliminary for
this first chapter of Śankara's teaching, the "four Perfections" should be learned by heart and taken to heart.

The Crest-Jewel of Wisdom

VIVEKACHÛDÂMANI

First Steps on the Path

(Verses 1 — 15)

I BOW before Govinda, the objectless object of final success in the highest wisdom, who is supreme bliss and the true teacher.

For beings a human birth is hard to win, then manhood and holiness, then excellence in the path of wise law; hardest of all to win is wisdom. Discernment between Self and not-Self, true judgment, nearness to the Self of the Eternal and Freedom are not gained without a myriad of right acts in a hundred births. This triad that is won by the bright one's favor is hard to gain: humanity, aspiration, and rest in the great spirit. After gaining at last a human birth, hard to win, then manhood and knowledge of the teaching, if one strives not after Freedom he is a fool. He, suicidal, destroys himself by grasping after the unreal. Who is more self-deluded than he who is careless of his own welfare after gaining a hard-won human birth and manhood, too? Let them declare the laws, let them offer to the gods, let them perform all rites, let them love the gods; without knowing the oneness with the Self, Freedom is not won even in a hundred years of the Evolver. "There is no hope of immortality through riches," says the scripture. It is clear from this that rites cannot lead to Freedom.

Therefore let the wise one strive after Freedom,

giving up all longing for sensual self-indulgence; approaching the good, great Teacher (the Higher Self), with soul intent on the object of the teaching. Let him by the Self raise the Self, sunk in the ocean of the world, following the path of union through complete recognition of oneness. Setting all rites aside, let the wise, learned ones who approach the study of the Self strive for Freedom from the bondage of the world. Rites are to purify the thoughts, but not to gain the reality. The real is gained by Wisdom, not by a myriad of rites. When one steadily examines and clearly sees a rope, the fear that it is a serpent is destroyed. Knowledge is gained by discernment, by examining, by instruction, but not by bathing, nor gifts, nor a hundred holdings of the breath. Success demands first ripeness; questions of time and place are subsidiary. Let the seeker after self-knowledge find the Teacher (the Higher Self), full of kindness and knowledge of the Eternal.

THE FOUR PERFECTIONS
(Verses 16 — 34)

He is ripe to seek the Self who is full of knowledge and wisdom, reason and discernment, and who bears the well-known marks.

He is ready to seek the Eternal who has Discernment and Dispassion; who has Restfulness and the other graces.

Four perfections are numbered by the wise. When they are present there is success, but in their absence is failure.

First is counted the Discernment between things

lasting and unlasting. Next Dispassion, the indifference to self-indulgence here and in paradise. Then the Six Graces, beginning with Restfulness. Then the longing for Freedom.

A certainty like this — the Eternal is real, the fleeting world is unreal; — this is that Discernment between things lasting and unlasting.

And this is Dispassion — a perpetual willingness to give up all sensual self-indulgence — everything lower than the Eternal, through a constant sense of their insufficiency.

Then the Six Graces: a steady intentness of the mind on its goal; — this is Restfulness.

And the steadying of the powers that act and perceive, each in its own sphere, turning them back from sensuality; — this is Self-control.

Then the raising of the mind above external things; — this is the true Withdrawal.

The enduring of all ills without petulance and without self-pity; — this is the right Endurance.

An honest confidence in the teaching and the Teacher; — this is that Faith by which the treasure is gained.

The intentness of the soul on the pure Eternal; — this is right Meditation, but not the indulgence of fancy.

The wish to untie, by discernment of their true nature, all the bonds woven by unwisdom, the bonds of selfishness and sensuality; — this is the longing for Freedom.

Though at first imperfect, these qualities gradually growing through Dispassion, Restfulness, and the other graces and the Teacher's help will gain their due.

When Dispassion and longing for Freedom are strong, then Restfulness and the other graces will bear fruit.

But when these two — Dispassion and longing for Freedom — are lacking, then Restfulness and the other graces are a mere appearance, like water in the desert.

Chief among the causes of Freedom is devotion, the intentness of the soul on its own nature. Or devotion may be called intentness on the reality of the Self.

Let him who possesses these Perfections and who would learn the reality of the Self, approach the wise Teacher (the Higher Self), from whom comes the loosing of bonds; who is full of knowledge and perfect; who is not beaten by desire, who really knows the Eternal; who has found rest in the Eternal, at peace like a fuelless fire; who is full of selfless kindness, the friend of all that lives. Serving the Teacher with devotion and aspiration for the Eternal, and finding harmony with him, seek the needed knowledge of the Self.

The Appeal to the Higher Self

(Verses 35 — 40)

"I submit myself to thee, Master, friend of the bowed-down world and river of selfless kindness.

"Raise me by thy guiding light that pours forth the nectar of truth and mercy, for I am sunk in the ocean of the world.

"I am burned by the hot flame of relentless life and torn by the winds of misery: save me from death, for I take refuge in thee, finding no other rest."

The great good ones dwell in peace, bringing joy to the world like the return of spring. Having crossed the ocean of the world, they ever help others to cross over.

For this is the very nature of the great-souled ones (Mahâtmas) — their swiftness to take away the weariness of others. So the soft-rayed moon of itself soothes the earth, burned by the fierce sun's heat.

"Sprinkle me with thy nectar voice that brings the joy of eternal bliss, pure and cooling, falling on me as from a cup, like the joy of inspiration; for I am burnt by the hot, scorching flames of the world's fire.

"Happy are they on whom thy light rests, even for a moment, and who reach harmony with thee.

"How shall I cross the ocean of the world? Where is the path? What way must I follow? I know not, Master. Save me from the wound of the world's pain."

THE BEGINNING OF THE TEACHING

(Verses 41 — 71)

To him, making this appeal and seeking help, scorched by the flame of the world's fire, the Great Soul beholding him with eyes most pitiful brings speedy comfort.

The Wise One instils the truth in him who has approached him longing for Freedom, who is following the true path, calming the tumult of his mind and bringing Restfulness.

"Fear not, wise one, there is no danger for thee. There is a way to cross over the ocean of the world, and by this path the sages have reached the shore.

"This same path I point out to thee, for it is the way to destroy the world's fear. Crossing the ocean of the world by this path, thou shalt win the perfect joy."

By discerning the aim of the wisdom-teaching (Vedânta) is born that most excellent knowledge. Then comes the final ending of the world's pain. The voice of the teaching plainly declares that faith, devotion, meditation, and the search for union are the means of Freedom for him who would be free. He who is perfect in these wins Freedom from the bodily bondage woven by unwisdom.

When the Self is veiled by unwisdom there arises a binding to the not-self, and from this comes the pain of world-life. The fire of wisdom lit by discernment between these two — Self and not-Self — will wither up the source of unwisdom, root and all.

THE PUPIL ASKS

"Hear with selfless kindness, Master. I ask this question: receiving the answer from thy lips I shall gain my end.

"What is, then, a bond? And how has this bond come? What cause has it? And how can one be free?

"What is not-Self and what the Higher Self? And how can one discern between them?"

THE MASTER ANSWERS

"Happy art thou. Thou shalt attain thy end. Thy kin is blest in thee. For thou seekest to become the Eternal by freeing thyself from the bond of unwisdom.

"Sons and kin can pay a father's debts, but none but a man's self can set him free.

"If a heavy burden presses on the head others can remove it, but none but a man's self can quench his hunger and thirst.

"Health is gained by the sick who follow the path of healing: health does not come through the acts of others.

"The knowledge of the real by the eye of clear insight is to be gained by one's own sight and not by the teacher's.

"The moon's form must be seen by one's own eyes; it can never be known through the eyes of another.

"None but a man's self is able to untie the knots of unwisdom, desire, and former acts, even in a myriad of ages.

"Freedom is won by a perception of the Self's oneness with the Eternal, and not by the doctrines of Union or of Numbers, nor by rites and sciences.

"The form and beauty of the lyre and excellent skill upon its strings may give delight to the people, but will never found an empire.

"An eloquent voice, a stream of words, skill in explaining the teaching, and the learning of the learned; these bring enjoyment but not freedom.

"When the Great Reality is not known the study of the scriptures is fruitless; when the Great Reality is known the study of the scriptures is also fruitless.

"A net of words is a great forest where the fancy wanders; therefore the reality of the Self is to be strenuously learned from the knower of that reality.

"How can the hymns (Vedas) and the scriptures profit him who is bitten by the serpent of unwisdom?

How can charms or medicine help him without the
medicine of the knowledge of the Eternal?

"Sickness is not cured by saying 'Medicine,' but by
drinking it. So a man is not set free by the name of
the Eternal without discerning the Eternal.

"Without piercing through the visible, without knowing the reality of the Self, how can men gain Freedom
by mere outward words that end with utterances?

"Can a man be king by saying, 'I am king,' without
destroying his enemies, without gaining power over the
whole land?

"Through information, digging, and casting aside the
stones, a treasure may be found, but not by calling it
to come forth.

"So by steady effort is gained the knowledge of those
who know the Eternal, the lonely, stainless reality
above all illusion; but not by desultory study.

"Hence with all earnest effort to be free from the
bondage of the world, the wise must strive themselves,
as they would to be free from sickness.

"And this question put by thee to-day must be solved
by those who seek Freedom; this question that breathes
the spirit of the teaching, that is like a clue with hidden
meaning.

"Hear, then, earnestly, thou wise one, the answer
given by me; for understanding it thou shalt be free
from the bondage of the world."

Self, Potencies, Vestures

THE first cause of Freedom is declared to be an utter turning back from lust after unenduring things. Thereafter Restfulness, Control, Endurance; a perfect Renouncing of all acts that cling and stain.

Thereafter, the divine Word, a turning of the mind to it, a constant thinking on it by the pure one, long and uninterrupted.

Then ridding himself altogether of doubt, and reaching wisdom, even here he enjoys the bliss of Nirvâna.

Then the discerning between Self and not-Self that you must now awaken to, that I now declare, hearing it, lay hold on it within yourself.

THE VESTURES

(Verses 72 — 107)

Formed of the substances they call marrow, bone, fat, flesh, blood, skin and over-skin; fitted with greater and lesser limbs, feet, breast, trunk, arms, back, head; this is called the physical vesture by the wise — the vesture whose authority, as "I" and "my" is declared to be a delusion.

Then these are the refined elements: the ethereal, the upper air, the flaming, water, and earth.

These when mingled one with another become the physical elements, that are the causes of the physical vesture. The materials of them become the five sensuous things that are for the delight of the enjoyer — sounds and other things of sense.

They who, fooled in these sensuous things, are bound by the wide noose of lust, hard to break asunder — they come and go, downwards and upwards on high, led by the swift messenger, their works.

Through the five sensuous things five creatures find dissolution to the five elements, each one bound by his own character: the deer, the elephant, the moth, the fish, the bee; what then of man, who is snared by all the five?

Sensuous things are keener to injure than the black snake's venom; poison slays only him who eats it, but these things slay only him who beholds them with his eyes.

He who is free from the great snare, so hard to be rid of, of longing after sensuous things, he indeed builds for Freedom, and not another, even though knowing the six philosophies.

Those who, only for a little while rid of lust, long to be free, and struggle to reach the shore of the world-ocean — the toothed beast of longing lust makes them sink half way, seizing them by the throat, and swiftly carrying them away.

By whom this toothed beast called sensuous things is slain by the sharp sword of true turning away from lust, he reaches the world-sea's shore without hindrance. He who, soul-destroyed, treads the rough path of sensuous things, death is his reward, like him who goes out on a luckless day. But he who goes onward, through the word of the good Teacher who is friendly to all beings, and himself well-controlled, he gains the fruit and the reward, and his reward is the Real.

If the love of Freedom is yours, then put sensuous things far away from you, like poison. But love, as the food of the gods, serenity, pity, pardon, rectitude, peacefulness and self-control; love them and honor them forever.

He who every moment leaving undone what should be done — the freeing of himself from the bonds of beginningless unwisdom — devotes himself to the fattening of his body, that rightly exists for the good of the other powers, such a one thereby destroys himself.

He who seeks to behold the Self, although living to fatten his body, is going to cross the river, holding to a toothed beast, while thinking it a tree.

For this delusion for the body and its delights is a great death for him who longs for Freedom; the delusion by the overcoming of which he grows worthy of the dwelling-place of the free.

Destroy this great death, this infatuation for the body, wives and sons; conquering it, the pure ones reach the Pervader's supreme abode.

This faulty form, built up of skin and flesh, of blood and sinews, fat and marrow and bones, gross and full of impure elements;

Born of the fivefold physical elements through deeds done before, the physical place of enjoyment of the Self; its mode is waking life, whereby there arises experience of physical things.

Subservient to physical objects through the outer powers, with its various joys — flower-chaplets, sandal, lovers — the Life makes itself like this through the power of the Self; therefore this form is pre-eminent in waking life.

But know that this physical body wherein the whole circling life of the Spirit adheres, is but as the dwelling of the lord of the dwelling.

Birth and age and death are the fate of the physical and all the physical changes from childhood onward; of the physical body only are caste and grade with their many homes, and differences of worship and dishonor and great honor belong to it alone.

The powers of knowing — hearing, touch, sight, smell, taste — for apprehending sensuous things; the powers of doing — voice, hands, feet, the powers that put forth and generate — to effect deeds.

Then the inward activity: mind, soul, self-assertion, imagination, with their proper powers; mind, ever intending and doubting; soul, with its character of certainty as to things; self-assertion, that falsely attributes the notion of "I"; imagination, with its power of gathering itself together, and directing itself to its object.

These also are the life-breaths: the forward-life, the downward-life, the distributing-life, the uniting-life; their activities and forms are different, as gold and water are different.

The subtle vesture they call the eightfold inner being made up thus: voice and the other four, hearing and the other four, ether and the other four, the forward life and the other four, soul and the other inward activities, unwisdom, desire, and action.

Hear now about this subtle vesture or form vesture,

born of elements not fivefolded; it is the place of gratification, the enjoyer of the fruits of deeds, the beginningless disguise of the Self, through lack of self-knowledge.

Dream-life is the mode of its expansion, where it shines with reflected light, through the traces of its own impressions; for in dream-life the knowing soul shines of itself through the many and varied mind-pictures made during waking-life.

Here the higher self shines of itself and rules, taking on the condition of doer, with pure thought as its disguise, an unaffected witness, nor is it stained by the actions, there done, as it is not attached to them, therefore it is not stained by actions, whatever they be, done by its disguise; let this form-vesture be the minister, doing the work of the conscious self, the real man, just as the tools do the carpenter's work; thus this self remains unattached.

Blindness or slowness or skill come from the goodness or badness of the eye; deafness and dumbness are of the ear and not of the Knower, the Self.

Up-breathing, down-breathing, yawning, sneezing, the forward moving of breath, and the outward moving — these are the doings of the life-breaths, say those who know these things; of the life-breaths, also, hunger and thirst are properties.

The inner activity dwells and shines in sight and the other powers in the body, through the false attribution of selfhood, as cause.

Self-assertion is to be known as the cause of this false attribution of selfhood, as doer and enjoyer; and through substance and the other two potencies, it reaches expansion in the three modes.

When sensuous things have affinity with it, it is happy; when the contrary, unhappy. So happiness and unhappiness are properties of this, and not of the Self which is perpetual bliss.

Sensuous things are dear for the sake of the self, and not for their own sake; and therefore the Self itself is dearest of all.

Hence the Self itself is perpetual bliss — not for it are happiness and unhappiness; as in dreamless life, where are no sensuous things, the Self that is bliss — is enjoyed, so in waking-life it is enjoyed through the word, through intuition, teaching and deduction.

The Three Potencies

(Verses 108 — 135)

The power of the supreme Master, that is called unmanifested, beginningless unwisdom whose very self is the three potencies, to be known through thought, by its workings — this is glamor (Mâyâ), whereby all this moving world is made to grow.

Neither being nor non-being nor of the self of both of these; neither divided nor undivided nor of the self of both of these; neither formed nor formless nor of the self of both of these — very wonderful and ineffable is its form.

To be destroyed by the awakening to the pure, secondless Eternal, as the serpent imagined in a rope, when the rope is seen; its potencies are called substance, force, and darkness; each of them known by their work-

ings. The self of doing belongs to force, whose power
is extension, whence the pre-existent activities issued;
rage and all the changes of the mind that cause sorrow
are ever its results.

Desire, wrath, greed, vanity, malice, self-assertion,
jealousy, envy, are the terrible works of Force, its activities in man; therefore this is the cause of bondage.

Then enveloping is the power of Darkness, whereby
a thing appears as something else; this is the cause of
the circling birth and rebirth of the spirit, and the
cause whereby extension is drawn forward.

Though a man be full of knowledge, learned, skill-
ful, very subtle-sighted, if Darkness has wrapped him
round, he sees not, though he be full of manifold instruction; he calls good that which is raised by error,
and leans upon its properties, unlucky man that he is;
great and hard to end is the enveloping power of Darkness.

Wrong thinking, contradictory thinking, fanciful
thinking, confused thinking — these are its workings;
this power of extension never leaves hold of one who
has come into contact with it, but perpetually sends
him this way and that.

Unwisdom, sluggishness, inertness, sloth, infatuation,
folly, and things like these are of the potency of Darkness. Under the yoke of these he knows nothing at
all, but remains as though asleep or like a post.

But the potency of substance is pure like water, and
even though mixed with the other two, it builds for the
true refuge; for it is a reflected spark of the Self, and
lights up the inert like the sun.

2) Of the potency of Substance when mixed the properties are self-respect, self-restraint, control, faith and
love and the longing to be free, a godlike power and a
turning back from the unreal.

3 Of the potency of substance altogether pure the properties are grace, direct perception of the Self, and perfect peace; exulting gladness, a resting on the Self
supreme, whereby he reaches the essence of real bliss.

The unmanifest is characterized by these three potencies; it is the causal vesture of the Self; dreamless
life is the mode where it lives freely, all the activities
of the powers, and even of the knowing soul having
sunk back into it.

Every form of outward perceiving has come to rest,
the knowing soul becomes latent in the Self from which
it springs; the name of this is dreamless life, wherein
he says "I know nothing at all of the noise of the moving world."

The body, powers, life-breaths, mind, self-assertion,
all changes, sensuous things, happiness, unhappiness,
the ether and all the elements, the whole world up to
the unmanifest — this is not Self.

Glamor and every work of glamor from the world-
soul to the body, know this as unreal, as not the Self,
built up of the mirage of the desert.

But I shall declare to you the own being of the Self
supreme, knowing which a man, freed from his bonds,
reaches the lonely purity.

There is a certain selfhood wherein the sense of "I"
forever rests; who witnesses the three modes of being,
who is other than the five veils; who is the only knower

in waking, dreaming, dreamlessness; of all the activities of the knowing soul, whether good or bad — this
is the "I";

Who of himself beholds all; whom none beholds;
who kindles to consciousness the knowing soul and all
the powers; whom none kindles to consciousness; by
whom all this is filled; whom no other fills; who is the
shining light within this all; after whose shining all
else shines;

By whose nearness only body and powers and mind
and soul do their work each in his own field, as though
sent by the Self;

Because the own nature of this is eternal wakefulness, self-assertion, the body and all the powers, and
happiness and unhappiness are beheld by it, just as an
earthen pot is beheld. This inner Self, the ancient
Spirit, is everlasting, partless, immediately experienced
happiness; ever of one nature, pure waking knowledge,
sent forth by whom Voice and the life-breaths move.

Here, verily, in the substantial Self, in the hidden
place of the soul, this steady shining begins to shine like
the dawn; then the shining shines forth as the noonday
sun, making all this world to shine by its inherent light;
knower of all the changing moods of mind and inward
powers; of all the acts done by body, powers, life-
breaths; present in them as fire in iron, strives not nor
changes at all.

This is not born nor dies nor grows, nor does it fade
or change forever; even when this form has melted
away, it no more melts than the air in a jar.

Alike stranger to forming and deforming; of its own

being, pure wakefulness; both being and non-being is
this, besides it there is nothing else; this shines unchanging, this Supreme Self gleams in waking, dream
and dreamlessness as "I," present as the witness of the
knowing soul.

BONDAGE AND FREEDOM

(Verses 136 — 153)

Then, holding firmly mind, with knowing soul at rest,
know your self within yourself face to face saying,
"This am I." The life-ocean, whose waves are birth
and dying, is shoreless; cross over it, fulfilling the end
of being, resting firm in the Eternal.

Thinking things not self are "I" — this is bondage
for a man; this, arising from unwisdom, is the cause of
falling into the weariness of birth and dying; this is
the cause that he feeds and anoints and guards this
form, thinking it the Self; the unreal, real; wrapping
himself in sensuous things as a silk-worm in his own
threads.

The thought that what is not That is That grows up
in the fool through darkness; because no discernment
is there, it wells up, as the thought that a rope is a
snake; thereupon a mighty multitude of fatuities fall
on him who accepts this error, for he who grasps the
unreal is bound; mark this, my companion.

By the power of wakefulness, partless, external, secondless, the Self wells up with its endless lordship; but
this enveloping power wraps it round, born of Darkness, as the dragon of eclipse envelops the rayed sun.

When the real Self with its stainless light recedes, a

man thinking "this body is I," calls it the Self; then by lust and hate and all the potencies of bondage, the great power of Force that they call extension greatly afflicts him.

Torn by the gnawing of the toothed beast of great delusion; wandered from the Self, accepting every changing mood of mind as himself, through this potency, in the shoreless ocean of birth and death, full of the poison of sensuous things, sinking and rising, he wanders, mean-minded, despicable-minded.

As a line of clouds, born of the sun's strong shining, expands before the sun and hides it from sight, so self-assertion, that has come into being through the Self, expands before the Self and hides it from sight. As when on an evil day the lord of day is swallowed up in thick, dark clouds, an ice-cold hurricane of wind, very terrible, afflicts the clouds in turns; so when the Self is enveloped in impenetrable Darkness, the keen power of extension drives with many afflictions the man whose soul is deluded.

From those two powers a man's bondage comes; deluded by them he errs, thinking the body is the Self.

Of the plant of birth and death, the seed is Darkness, the sprout is the thought that body is Self, the shoot is rage, the sap is deeds, the body is the stem, the life-breaths are the branches, the tops are the bodily powers, sensuous things are the flowers, sorrow is the fruit, born of varied deeds and manifold; and the Life is the bird that eats the fruit.

This bondage to what is not Self, rooted in unwisdom, innate, made manifest without beginning or end, gives life to the falling torrent of sorrow, of birth and death, of sickness and old age.

Not by weapons nor arms, not by storm nor fire nor by a myriad deeds can this be cut off, without the sword of discernment and knowledge, very sharp and bright, through the grace of the guiding power.

He who is single-minded, fixed on the word divine, his steadfast fulfilment of duty will make the knowing soul within him pure; to him whose knowing soul is pure, a knowing of the Self supreme shall come; and through this knowledge of the Self supreme he shall destroy this circle of birth and death and its root together.

THE FREEING OF THE SELF

(Verses 148 — 154)

The Self, wrapped up in the five vestures beginning with the vesture formed of food, which are brought into being by its own power, does not shine forth, as the water in the pond, covered by a veil of green scum.

When the green scum is taken away, immediately the water shines forth pure, taking away thirst and heat, straightway becoming a source of great joy to man.

When the five vestures have been stripped off, the Self shines forth pure, the one essence of eternal bliss, beheld within, supreme, self-luminous.

Discernment is to be made between the Self and what is not Self by the wise man seeking freedom from bondage; through this he enters into joy, knowing the Self which is being, consciousness, bliss.

As the reed from the tiger grass, so separating from the congeries of things visible the hidden Self within, which is detached, not involved in actions, and dissolving all in the Self, he who stands thus, has attained liberation.

THE VESTURE FORMED OF FOOD

(Verses 154 — 164)

The food-formed vesture is this body, which comes into being through food, which lives by food, which perishes without food.

It is formed of cuticle, skin, flesh, blood, bone, water; this is not worthy to be the Self, eternally pure.

The Self was before birth or death, and now is; how can it be born for the moment, fleeting, unstable of nature, not unified, inert, beheld like a jar? For the Self is the witness of all changes of form.

The body has hands and feet, not the Self; though bodiless, yet because it is the Life, because its power is indestructible, it is controller, not controlled.

Since the Self is witness of the body, its character, its acts, its states, therefore the Self must be of other nature than the body.

A mass of wretchedness, clad in flesh, full of impurity and evil, how can this body be the knower? The Self is of other nature.

Of this compound of skin, flesh, fat, bone and water, the man of deluded mind thinks, "This is I"; but he who is possessed of judgment knows that his true Self is of other character, is nature transcendental.

The mind of the dullard thinks of the body, "This is I"; he who is more learned thinks, "This is I," of the body and the separate self; but he who has attained discernment and is wise knows the true Self saying, "I am the Eternal."

Therefore, O thou of mind deluded, put away the thought that this body is the Self, this compound of skin, flesh, fat, bone and water; discern the universal Self, the Eternal, changeless, and enjoy supreme peace.

So long as the man of learning abandons not the thought, founded on delusion, that "This is I," regarding the unenduring body and its powers, so long there is no hope for his liberation, though he possess the knowledge of the Vedânta and its sciences.

As thou hast no thought that "This is the Self," regarding the body's shadow, or the reflected form, or the body seen in dream, or the shape imagined in the mind, so let not this thought exist regarding the living body.

The thought that the body is the Self, in the minds of men who discern not the real, is the seed from which spring birth and death and sorrow; therefore slay thou this thought with strong effort, for when thou hast abandoned this thought the longing for rebirth will cease.

THE VESTURE FORMED OF VITAL BREATH

(Verses 165 — 166)

The breath-formed vesture is formed by the life-breath determined by the five powers of action; through its power the food-formed vesture, guided by the Self and sustained by food, moves in all bodily acts.

Nor is this breath-formed vesture the Self, since it is formed of the vital airs, coming and going like the wind, moving within and without; since it can in no

wise discern between right and wrong, between oneself
and another, but is ever dependent.

3 THE VESTURE FORMED OF MIND

(Verses 167 — 183)

The mind-formed vesture is formed of the powers of
perception and the mind; it is the cause of the distinction between the notions of "mine" and "I"; it is active in making a distinction of names and numbers; as
more potent, it pervades and dominates the former
vesture.

The fire of the mind-formed vesture, fed by the five
powers of perception, as though by five sacrificial
priests, with objects of sense like streams of melted
butter, blazing with the fuel of manifold sense-impres-
sions, sets the personality aflame.

For there is no unwisdom, except in the mind, for
the mind is unwisdom, the cause of the bondage to life;
when this is destroyed, all is destroyed; when this
dominates, the world dominates.

In dream, devoid of substance, it emanates a world
of experiencer and things experienced, which is all
mind; so in waking consciousness, there is no difference,
it is all the domination of the mind.

During the time of dreamlessness, when mind has
become latent, nothing at all of manifestation remains;
therefore man's circle of birth and death is built by
mind, and has no permanent reality.

By the wind a cloud is collected, by the wind it is
driven away again; by mind bondage is built up, by
mind is built also liberation.

I am not this mind and its Illusions
Mother, please detach me from this
mind and its Maya
I am not these desires They are not mine
Please free me from the poison of the mind in
the form of de-
sires, passion
please dispell
the darkness
and passion
of this mind

Building up desire for the body and all objects, it binds the man thereby as an ox by a cord; afterwards leading him to turn from them like poison, that same mind, verily, sets him free from bondage.

Therefore mind is the cause of man's bondage, and in turn of his liberation; when darkened by the powers of passion it is the cause of bondage, and when pure of passion and darkness it is the cause of liberation.

Where discernment and dispassion are dominant, gaining purity, the mind makes for liberation; therefore let the wise man who seeks liberation strengthen these two in himself as the first step.

Mind is the name of the mighty tiger that hunts in the forest glades of sensuous things; let not the wise go thither, who seek liberation.

Mind moulds all sensuous things through the earthly body and the subtle body of him who experiences; mind ceaselessly shapes the differences of body, of color, of condition, of race, as fruits caused by the acts of the potencies.

Mind, beclouding the detached, pure consciousness, binding it with the cords of the body, the powers, the life-breaths, as "I" and "my," ceaselessly strays among the fruits of experience caused by its own activities.

Man's circle of birth and death comes through the fault of attributing reality to the unreal, but this false attribution is built up by mind; this is the effective cause of birth and death and sorrow for him who has the faults of passion and darkness and is without discernment.

Therefore the wise who know the truth have declared

that mind is unwisdom, through which the whole
world, verily, is swept about, as cloud belts by the wind.

Therefore purification of the mind should be undertaken with strong effort by him who seeks liberation;
when the mind has been purified, liberation comes like
fruit into his hand.

Through the sole power of liberation uprooting desire for sensuous things, and ridding himself of all
bondage to works, he who through faith in the Real
stands firm in the teaching, shakes off the very essence
of passion from the understanding.

The mind-formed vesture cannot be the higher Self,
since it has beginning and end, waxing and waning;
by causing sensuous things, it is the very essence of
pain; that which is itself seen cannot be the Seer.

The Vesture formed of Intelligence

(Verses 184 — 197)

The intelligence, together with the powers of intelligence, makes the intelligence-formed vesture, whose
distinguishing character is actorship; it is the cause of
man's circle of birth and death.

The power which is a reflected beam of pure Consciousness, called the understanding, is a mode of abstract Nature; it possesses wisdom and creative power;
it thereby focuses the idea of "I" in the body and its
powers.

This "I," beginningless in time, is the separate self,
it is the initiator of all undertakings; this, impelled by
previous imprints, works all works both holy and un-
holy, and forms their fruits.

Passing through varying births it gains experience, now descending, now ascending; of this intelligence-formed vesture, waking, dream and dreamlessness are the fields where it experiences pleasure and pain.

By constantly attributing to itself the body, state, condition, duties and works, thinking, "These are mine," this intelligence-formed vesture, brightly shining because it stands closest to the higher Self, becomes the vesture of the Self, and, thinking itself to be the Self, wanders in the circle of birth and death.

This, formed of intelligence, is the light that shines in the vital breaths, in the heart; the Self who stands forever wears this vesture as actor and experiencer.

The Self, assuming the limitation of the intelligence, self-deluded by the error of the intelligence, though it is the universal Self, yet views itself as separate from the Self; as the potter views the jars as separate from the clay.

Through the force of its union with the vesture, the higher Self takes on the character of the vesture and assumes its nature, as fire, which is without form, takes on the varying forms of the iron, even though the Self is for ever by nature uniform and supreme.

The Disciple Speaks

Whether by delusion or otherwise, the higher Self appears as the separate self; but, since the vesture is beginningless, there is no conceivable end of the beginningless.

Therefore existence as the separate self must be eternal, nor can the circle of birth and death have an end; how then can there be liberation?   Master, tell me this.

THE MASTER ANSWERS

Well hast thou asked, O wise one!   Therefore rightly hear!   A false imagination created by error is not conclusive proof.

Only through delusion can there be an association with objects, of that which is without attachment, without action, without form; it is like the association of blueness with the sky.

The appearance as the separate self, of the Self, the Seer, who is without qualities, without form; essential wisdom and bliss, arises through the delusion of the understanding; it is not real; when the delusion passes, it exists no longer, having no substantial reality.

Its existence, which is brought into being through false perception, because of delusion, lasts only so long as the error lasts; as the serpent in the rope endures only as long as the delusion; when the delusion ceases, there is no serpent.

when the delusion ceases there is no serpent →

The Witness

THE MANIFEST AND THE HIDDEN SELF

(Verses 198 — 209)

Unwisdom

BEGINNINGLESS is unwisdom, and all its works are too; but when wisdom is arisen, what belongs to unwisdom, although beginningless —

Like a dream on waking, perishes, root and all; though beginningless, it is not endless; it is as something that was not before, *and now is,* this is manifest.

It is thus seen that, though without a beginning, *unwisdom* comes to an end, just as something, which before was not, *comes into being.* Built up in the Self by its being bound by disguise of intellect —

Is this existence as the *separate* life, for there is no other than the Self, distinguished by its own nature, but the binding of the Self by the intellect is false, coming from unknowledge.

This binding is untied by perfect knowledge, not otherwise; the discerning of the oneness of the Eternal and the Self is held by the scripture to be perfect knowledge.

And this is accomplished by perfectly discerning between Self and not-self; thereafter discernment is to be gained between individual and universal Self.

Water may be endlessly muddy, but when the mud is gone, the water is clear. As it shines, so shines the Self also, when faults are gone away, it shines forth clear.

And when unreality ceases to exist in the individual self, it is clear that it returns towards the universal;

hence there is to be a rejection of the self-assertion and other characteristics of the individual self.

Hence this higher Self is not what is called the intellectual veil, because that is changeful, helpless of itself, circumscribed, objective, liable to err; the non-eternal cannot be regarded as eternal.

The bliss-formed veil is a form containing the reflection of bliss — although it is tainted with darkness; it has the quality of pleasure, the attainment of well wished-for aims; it shines forth in the enjoyment of good works by a righteous man, of its own nature bliss-formed; gaining an excellent form, he enjoys bliss without effort.

The principal sphere of the bliss-formed veil is in dreamless sleep; in dreaming and waking it is in part manifest when blissful objects are beheld.

Nor is this bliss-formed veil the higher Self, for it wears a disguise, it is a form of objective nature; it is an effect caused by good acts, accumulated in this changeful form.

When the five veils are taken away, according to inference and scripture, what remains after they are taken away is the Witness, in a form born of awakening.

This is the Self, self-shining, distinguished from the five veils; this is the Witness in the three modes *of perceiving*, without change, without stain. The wise should know it as Being and Bliss, as his own Self.

THE PUPIL SAID:

(Verses 210 — 240)

When the five veils are thus set aside through their

unreality, beyond the non-being of all I see nothing, Master; what then is to be known as anything by him who knows Self and not-self?

THE MASTER SAID:

Truth has been spoken by thee, wise one; thou art skilled in judgment. Self-assertion and all these changes, — in the Self they have no being. That whereby all is enjoyed, but which is itself not enjoyed, know that to be the Self, the Knower, through thy very subtle intellect.

Whatever is enjoyed by anyone, of that he is the witness; but of that which is not enjoyed by anyone, it cannot be said that anyone is the witness.

That is to be self-witness, where anything is enjoyed by itself; therefore the universal Self is witness of itself; no other lesser thing is witness of it.

In waking, dreaming, dreamlessness, that Self is clearly manifested, appearing through its universal form always as "I," as the "I" within, uniformly. This is "I" beholding intellect and the rest that partake of varied forms and changes. It is manifest through eternal blissful self-consciousness; know that as the Self here in the heart.

Looking at the reflection of the sun reflected in the water of a jar, he who is deluded thinks it is the sun, thus the reflected consciousness appearing under a disguise is thought by him who is hopelessly deluded to be "I."

Rejecting jar and water and the sun reflected there all together, the real sun is beheld. So the unchanging

One which is reflected in the three modes, self-shining,
is perceived by the wise.

Putting away in thought body and intellect as alike
reflections of consciousness, discerning the seer, hid
in the secret place, the Self, the partless awakening,
the universal shining, distinguished alike from what
exists and what does not exist; the eternal lord, all-
present, very subtle, devoid of within and without,
nothing but self; discerning this perfectly, in its own
form, a man is sinless, passionless, deathless.

Sorrowless, altogether bliss, full of wisdom, fearing
nothing at all from anything; there is no other path of
freedom from the bondage of the world but knowledge
of the reality of his Self, for him who would be free.

Knowledge that the Eternal is not divided *from him*
is the cause of freedom from the world, whereby the
Eternal, the secondless bliss, is gained by the awakened.

Therefore one should perfectly know that the Eternal
and the Self are not divided; for the wise who has become the Eternal does not return again to birth and
death.

The real, wisdom, the endless, the Eternal, pure,
supreme, self-perfect, the one essence of eternal bliss,
universal, undivided, unbroken — this he gains.

This is the real, supreme, secondless, for besides the
Self no other is; there is nothing else at all in the condition of perfect awakening to the reality of the supreme being.

This all, that is perceived as the vari-form world,
from unknowledge, this all is the Eternal, when the
mind's confusion is cast away.

The pot made of clay is not separate from the clay, for all through it is in its own nature clay; the form of the pot is not separate; whence then the pot?   It is mere name, built up of illusion.

By no one can the form of the pot be seen, separate from the clay; hence the pot is built of delusion, but the real thing is the clay, like the supreme Being.

All this is always an effect of the real Eternal; it is that alone, nor is there anything else but that. He who says there is, is not free from delusion, like one who talks in his sleep.

The Eternal verily is this all; thus says the excellent scripture of the *Atharva*.   In accordance with it, all this is the Eternal only, nor is there any separate existence of the attribute apart from the source.

If this moving world were the real, then had the Self no freedom from limitation, divine authority no worth, the Master Self no truth; these three things the great-souled cannot allow.

The Master who knows the reality of things declared: I verily am not contained in these things, nor do these creatures stand in me. If the world be real, then it should be apprehended in dreamless sleep; it is not apprehended there, therefore it is unreal, dream-like, false. Therefore the world is not separate from the higher Self; what is perceived as separate is false, — the natural potencies and the like; what real existence is there in the attribute? Its support shines forth *as with attributes* illusively.

Whatever is delusively perceived by one deluded, is the Eternal; the silver shining is only the pearl shell.

The Eternal is perpetually conceived as formed; but what is attributed to the Eternal is a name only.

Therefore the supreme Eternal is Being, secondless, of the form of pure knowledge, stainless, peaceful, free from beginning or ending, changeless, its own-nature is unbroken bliss.

Every difference made by world-glamor set aside, eternal, lasting, partless, measureless, formless, unmanifest, nameless, unfading, a self-shining light that illuminates all that is.

Where the difference of knower, knowing, known is gone, endless, sure; absolute, partless, pure consciousness; the wise know this as the supreme reality.

That can neither be left nor taken, is no object of mind or speech; immeasurable, beginningless, endless, the perfect Eternal, the universal "I."

That Thou Art

(Verses 241 — 251)

The Eternal and the Self, indicated by the two words "that" and "thou," when clearly understood, according to the Scripture "THAT THOU ART," are one; their oneness is again ascertained.

This identity of theirs is in their essential, not their verbal meanings, for they are *apparently* of contradictory character; like the firefly and the sun, the sovereign and the serf, the well and the great waters, the atom and Mount Meru.

The contradiction between them is built up by their disguises, but this disguise is no real thing at all; the disguise of the Master Self is the world-glamor, the cause of the Celestial and other worlds; the disguise of the *individual* life is the group of five veils — hear this now:

These are the two disguises, of the Supreme and the *individual* life; when they are set aside together, there is no longer the Supreme nor the *individual* life. The king has his kingdom, the warrior his weapons; when these are put away there is neither warrior nor king.

According to the Scripture saying, "this is the instruction, *the Self is not that, not that,*" the twofoldness that was built up sinks away of itself in the Eternal; let the truth of this scripture be grasped through awakening; the putting away of the two disguises must verily be accomplished.

It is not this, it is not this: because this is built up, it is not the real — like the serpent seen in the rope, or like a dream; thus putting away every visible thing by wise meditation, the oneness of the two — *Self and Eternal* — is then to be known.

Therefore the two are to be well observed in their essential unity. Neither their contradictory character nor their non-contradictory character is all; but the real and essential Being is to be reached, in order to gain the essence in which they are one and undivided.

When one says: "This man is Devadatta," the oneness is here stated by rejecting contradictory qualities. With the great word "THAT THOU ART," it is the same; what is contradictory between the two is set aside.

As being essentially pure consciousness, the oneness between the Real and the Self is known by the awakened; and by hundreds of great texts the oneness, the absence of separateness, between the Eternal and the Self is declared.

That is not the physical; it is the perfect, after the unreal is put aside; like the ether, not to be handled by thought. Hence this matter that is perceived is illusive, therefore set it aside; but what is grasped by its own selfhood — "that I am the Eternal" — know that with intelligence purified; know the Self as part-less awakening.

Every pot and vessel has always clay as its cause, and its material is clay; just like this, this world is en-gendered by the Real, and has the Real as its Self, the Real is its material altogether. That Real than which there is none higher, THAT THOU ART, the restful, the stainless, secondless Eternal, the supreme.

THE MANIFEST AND THE HIDDEN SELF *Become it in the Self.*

(Verses 252 — 268)

As dream-built lands and times, objects and knowers of them, are all unreal, just so here in waking is this world; its cause is ignorance of the Self; in as much as all this world, body and organs, vital breath and per-sonality are all unreal, in so much THOU ART THAT, the restful, the stainless, secondless Eternal, the supreme.

Far away from birth and conduct, family and tribe, quite free from name and form and quality and fault; beyond space and time and objects — this is the Eter-nal, THAT THOU ART; become it in the Self.

The supreme, that no word can reach, but that is reached by the eye of awakening, pure of stain, the pure reality of consciousness and mind together — this is the Eternal, THAT THOU ART; become it in the Self.

Untouched by the six infirmities, reached in the heart of those that seek for union, reached not by the organs, whose being neither intellect nor reason knows — this is the Eternal, THAT THOU ART; become it in the Self.

Built of error is the world; in That it rests; That rests in itself, different from the existent and the non-existent; partless, nor bound by causality, is the Eternal, THAT THOU ART; become it in the Self.

Birth and growth, decline and loss, sickness and death it is free from, and unfading; the cause of emanation, preservation, destruction, is the Eternal, THAT THOU ART; become it in the Self.

Where all difference is cast aside, all distinction is cast away, a waveless ocean, motionless; ever free, with undivided form — this is the Eternal, THAT THOU ART; become it in the Self.

Being one, though cause of many, the cause of others, with no cause itself; where cause and caused are merged in one, self-being, the Eternal, THAT THOU ART; become it in the Self.

Free from doubt and change, great, unchanging; where changing and unchanging are merged in one Supreme; eternal, unfading joy, unstained — this is the Eternal, THAT THOU ART; become it in the Self.

This shines forth manifold through error, through being the Self under name and form and quality and change; like gold itself unchanging ever — this is the Eternal, THAT THOU ART; become it in the Self.

This shines out unchanging, higher than the highest, the hidden one essence, whose character is selfhood, reality, consciousness, joy, endless unfading — this is the Eternal, THAT THOU ART; become it in the Self.

Let a man make it his own in the Self — like a word that is spoken, by reasoning from the known, by thought; this is as devoid of doubt as water in the hand, so certain will its reality become.

Recognizing this perfectly illumined one, whose reality is altogether pure, as *one recognizes* the leader of men in the assembled army, and resting on that always, standing firm in one's own Self, sink all this world that is born, into the Eternal.

In the soul, in the hidden place, marked neither as what is nor what is not, is the Eternal, true, supreme, secondless. He who through the Self dwells here in the secret place, for him there is no coming forth again to the world of form.

When the thing is well known even, this beginningless mode of thought, "I am the doer and the enjoyer," is very powerful; this mode of mind lasting strongly, is the cause of birth and rebirth. A looking backward toward the Self, a dwelling on it, is to be effortfully gained; freedom here on earth, say the saints, is the thinning away of that mode of thought.

That thought of 'I' and 'mine' in the flesh, the eye and the rest, that are not the Self — this transference *from the real to the unreal* is to be cast away by the wise man by steadfastness in his own Self.

Finding the Real Self

Recognizing as thine own the hidden Self, the witness of the soul and its activities, perceiving truly "That am I," destroy the thought of Self in all not Self.

Give up following after the world, give up following after the body, give up following after the ritual law; make an end of transferring selfhood to these.

Through a man's imagination being full of the world, through his imagination being full of the ritual law, through his imagination being full of the body, wisdom, truly, is not born in him.

For him who seeks freedom from the grasping hand of birth and death, an iron fetter binding his feet, say they who know it, is this potent triad of imaginings; he who has got free from this enters into freedom.

The scent of sandalwood that drives all evil odors away comes forth through stirring it with water and the like; all other odors are driven altogether away.

The image of the supreme Self, stained by the dust of imaginings, dwelling inwardly, endless, evil, comes forth pure, by the stirring power of enlightenment, as the scent of the sandalwood comes forth clear.

In the net of imaginings of things not Self, the image of the Self is held back; by resting on the eternal Self, their destruction comes, and the Self shines clear.

As the mind rests more and more on the Self behind

it, it is more and more freed from outward imaginings; when imaginings are put away, and no residue left, he enters and becomes the Self, pure of all bonds.

SELFHOOD TRANSFERRED TO THINGS NOT SELF

(Verses 277 — 298)

By resting ever in the Self, the restless mind of him who seeks union is stilled, and all imaginings fade away; therefore make an end of transferring Selfhood to things not Self.

Darkness is put away through force and substantial being; force, through substantial being; in the pure, substantial being is not put away; therefore, relying on substantial being, make an end of transferring Selfhood to things not Self.

The body of desire is nourished by all new works begun; steadily thinking on this, and effortfully holding desire firm, make an end of transferring selfhood to things not Self.

Thinking: "I am not this separate life but the supreme Eternal," beginning by rejecting all but this, make an end of transferring selfhood to things not Self; it comes from the swift impetus of imaginings.

Understanding the all-selfhood of the Self, by learning, seeking union, entering the Self, make an end of transferring selfhood to things not Self; it comes from the Self's reflected light in other things.

Neither in taking nor giving does the sage act at all; therefore by ever resting on the One, make an end of transferring selfhood to things not Self.

Through sentences like "That thou art" awaking to

the oneness of the Eternal and the Self, to confirm the Self in the Eternal, make an end of transferring selfhood to things not Self.

While there yet lingers a residue undissolved of the thought that this body is the Self, carefully seeking union with the Self, make an end of transferring selfhood to things not Self.

As long as the thought of separate life and the world shines, dreamlike even, so long incessantly, O wise one, make an end of transferring selfhood to things not Self.

The body of desire, born of father and mother of impure elements, made up of fleshly things impure, is to be abandoned as one abandons an impure man afar; gain thy end by becoming the Eternal.

The Real in Things Unreal

As the space in a jar in universal space, so the Self is to be merged without division in the Self supreme; rest thou ever thus, O sage.

Through the separate self gaining the Self, self-shining as a resting-place, let all outward things from a world-system to a lump of clay be abandoned, like a vessel of impure water.

Raising the thought of "I" from the body to the Self that is Consciousness, Being, Bliss, and lodging it there, leave form, and become pure for ever.

Knowing that "I am that Eternal" wherein this world is reflected, like a city in a mirror, thou shalt perfectly gain thy end.

What is of real nature, self-formed, original consciousness, secondless bliss, formless, actless — entering that, let a man put off this false body of desires, worn by the Self as a player puts on a costume.

For the Self, all that is seen is but mirage; it lasts but for a moment, we see, and know it is not "I"; how could "I know all" be said of the personal self that changes every moment?

The real "I" is witness of the personal self and its powers; as its being is perceived always, even in dreamless sleep. The scripture says the Self is unborn, everlasting; this is the hidden Self, distinguished neither as what exists nor what has no existence.

The beholder of every change in things that change, can be the unchanging alone; in the mind's desires, in dreams, in dreamless sleep the insubstantial nature of things that change is clearly perceived again and again.

Therefore put away the false selfhood of this fleshly body, for the false selfhood of the body is built up by thought; knowing the Self as thine own, unhurt by the three times, undivided illumination, enter into peace.

Put away the false selfhood of family and race and name, of form and rank, for these dwell in this body; put away the actorhood and other powers of the body of form; become the Self whose self is partless joy.

Other bonds of man are seen, causes of birth and death, but the root and first form of them is selfishness.

The Power of Mind-Images

A s long as the Self is in bondage to the false personal self of evil, so long is there not even a possibility of freedom, for these two are contraries.

But when free from the grasp of selfish personality, he reaches his real nature; Bliss and Being shine forth by their own light, like the full moon, free from blackness.

But he who in the body thinks "this am I," a delusion built up by the mind through darkness; when this delusion is destroyed for him without remainder, there arises for him the realization of Self as the Eternal, free from all bondage.

The treasure of the bliss of the Eternal is guarded by the terrible serpent of personality, very powerful, enveloping the Self, with three fierce heads — the three nature-powers; cutting off these three heads with the great sword of discernment, guided by the divine teachings, and destroying the serpent, the wise man may enter into that joy-bringing treasure.

So long as there is even a trace of the taint of poison in the body, how can there be freedom from sickness? In just the same way, there is no freedom for him who seeks union, while selfishness endures.

When the false self ceases utterly, and the motions of the mind caused by it come to an end, then, by discerning the hidden Self, the real truth that "I am that" is found.

Give up at once the thought of "I" in the action of the selfish personality, in the changeful self, which is but a reflection of the real Self, destroying rest in the Self; from falsely attributing reality to which are incurred birth and death and old age, fruitful in sorrow, the pilgrimage of the soul; but reality belongs to the hidden Self, whose form is consciousness, whose body is bliss; whose nature is ever one, the conscious Self, the Master, whose form is Bliss, whose glory is unspeakable; there is no cause of the soul's pilgrimage but the attribution of the reality of this to the selfish personality.

Therefore this selfish personality, the enemy of the Self, like a thorn in the throat of the eater, being cut away by the great sword of knowledge, thou shalt enjoy the bliss of the Self's sovereignty, according to thy desire.

Therefore bringing to an end the activity of the selfish personality, all passion being laid aside when the supreme object is gained, rest silent, enjoying the bliss of the Self, in the Eternal, through the perfect Self, from all doubt free.

Mighty selfishness, even though cut down root and all, if brought to life again even for a moment, in thought, causes a hundred dissipations of energy, as a cloud shaken by the wind in the rainy seasons, pours forth its floods.

After seizing the enemy, selfishness, no respite at all is to be given to it, by thoughts of sensual objects. Just this is the cause of its coming to life again, as water is of the lime tree that had withered away.   [310]

The desirer is constituted by the bodily self; how can the cause of desire be different? Hence the motion of enticement to sensual objects is the cause of world-bondage, through attachment to what is other than Self.

From increase of action, it is seen that the seed of bondage is energized; when action is destroyed, the seed is destroyed. Hence let him check sensual action.

From the growth of mind-images comes the action; from action the mind-image grows; hence the man's pilgrimage ceases not.

To cut the bonds of the world's pilgrimage, both must be burned away by the ascetic. And the growth of mind-images comes from these two — imagining and external action.

Growing from these two, it brings forth the pilgrimage of the soul. The way of destroying these three in every mode of consciousness, should be constantly sought.

By looking on all as the Eternal, everywhere, in every way, and by strengthening the mind-image of real being, this triad comes to melt away.

In the destruction of actions will arise the destruction of imaginings, and from this the dispersal of mind-images. The thorough dispersal of mind-images is freedom; this is called freedom even in life.

When the mind-image of the real grows up, in the dispersal of the mind's alarms, and the mind-image of the selfish personality melts away, as even thick darkness is quickly melted away before the light of the sun.

The action of the greatest darkness, the snare of

unreality, is no longer seen when the lord of day is arisen; so in the shining of the essence of secondless bliss, no bond exists nor scent of sorrow.

Transcending every visible object of sense, fixing the mind on pure being, the totality of bliss, with right intentness within and without, pass the time while the bonds of action last. [320]

Wavering in reliance on the Eternal must never be allowed; wavering is death — thus said the son of the Evolver.

There is no other danger for him who knows, but this wavering as to the Self's real nature. Thence arises delusion, and thence selfish personality; thence comes bondage, and therefrom sorrow.

Through beholding sensual objects, forgetfulness bewilders a wise man even, as a woman her favorite lover.

As sedge pushed back does not remain even for a moment, just in the same way does the world-glamor close over a wise man, who looks away from the Real.

If the imagination falling even a little from its aim, towards outward objects, it falls on and on, through unsteadiness, like a player's fallen on a row of steps.

If the thought enters into sensual objects, it becomes intent on their qualities; from this intentness immediately arises desire, and, from desire, every action of man.

Hence than this wavering there is no worse death, for one who has gained discernment, who has beheld the Eternal in spiritual concentration. By right intentness he at once gains success; be thou intent on the Self, with all carefulness.

Then comes loss of knowledge of one's real being, and he who has lost it falls; and destruction of him who thus falls is seen, but not restoration.

Let him put away the wilful motions of the mind, the cause of every evil act; he who has unity in life, has unity after his body is gone. The scripture of sentences says that he who beholds difference has fear.

Whenever even a wise man beholds difference in the endless Eternal, though only as much as an atom, what he beholds through wavering becomes a fear to him through its difference. [330]

All scripture, tradition and logic disregarding, whoever makes the thought of self in visible things, falls upon sorrow after sorrow; thus disregarding, he is like a thief in darkness.

He whose delight is attachment to the real, freed, he gains the greatness of the Self, eternal; but he who delights in attachment to the false, perishes; this is seen in the case of the thief and him who is no thief.

The ascetic, who has put away the cause of bondage — attachment to the unreal — stands in the vision of the Self, saying, "this Self am I"; this resting in the Eternal, brings joy by experiencing it, and takes away the supreme sorrow that we feel, whose cause is unwisdom.

Attachment to the outward brings as its fruit the perpetual increase of evil mind-images. Knowing this and putting away outward things by discernment, let him place his attachment in the Self forever.

When the outward is checked, there is restfulness from emotion; when emotion is at rest, there is vision of the supreme Self. When the Self is seen, the bond-

age of the world is destroyed; the checking of the outward is the path of freedom.

Who, being learned, discerning between real and unreal, knowing the teaching of the scripture, and beholding the supreme object with understanding, would place
his reliance on the unreal, even though longing to be
free — like a child, compassing his own destruction.

There is no freedom for him who is full of attachment to the body and its like; for him who is free, there
is no wish for the body and its like; the dreamer is not
awake, he who is awake dreams not; for these things
are the opposites of each other.

Knowing the Self as within and without, in things
stable and moving — discerning this through the Self,
through its comprehending all things — putting off
every disguise, and recognizing no division, standing
firm through the perfect Self — such a one is free.

Through the All-self comes the cause of freedom from
bondage; than the being of the All-self there is no other
cause; and this arises when there is no grasping after
the outer; he gains the being of the All-self by perpetually resting on the Self.

How should cessation of grasping after the outer not
fail for him who, through the bodily self remains with
mind attached to enjoyment of outward objects, and
thus engages in action. It can only be effortfully accomplished by those who have renounced the sensual
aims of all acts and rites, who are perfected in resting
on the eternal Self, who know reality, who long for
reality and bliss in the Self.   [340]

The scripture that speaks of "him who is at peace,

controlled," teaches the ecstasy of the ascetic, whose
work is the study of wisdom, to the end of gaining the
All-self.

The destruction of personality which has risen up in
power cannot be done at once, even by the learned,
except those who are immovably fixed in the ecstasy
which no doubt can assail, for the mind-images are of
endless rebirth.

Binding a man with the delusion of belief in his personality, through the power that veils, the power that
propels casts him forth, through its potencies.

The victory over this compelling power cannot be
accomplished, until the power that veils has come to
cessation with residue. The power that veils is, through
the force of its own nature, destroyed, when the seer
is discerned from what is seen, as milk is distinguished
from water.

Perfect discernment, born of clear awakening, arises
free from doubt, and pure of all bondage, where there
is no propelling power towards delusive objects, once
the division is made between the real natures of the
seer and what is seen; he cuts the bonds of delusion
that glamor makes, and, after that, there is no more pilgrimage for the free.

The flame of discernment of the oneness of the higher
and the lower, burns up the forest of unwisdom utterly.
What seed of the soul's pilgrimage can there be for him
who has gained being in which there is no duality?

And the cessation of the veiling power arises from
perfect knowledge; the destruction of false knowledge

is the cessation of the pain engendered by the propelling power.

The triple error is understood by knowing the real nature of the rope; therefore the reality of things is to be known by the wise to the end of freedom from bondage.

As iron from union with fire, so, from union with the real, thought expands as material things; hence the triple effect of this, seen in delusion, dream, desire, is but a mirage.

Thence come all changing forms in nature beginning with personality and ending with the body, and all sensual objects; these are unreal, because subject to change every moment; but the Self never changes. [350]

Consciousness, eternal, non-dual, partless, uniform, witness of intellect and the rest, different from existent and non-existent; its real meaning is the idea of "I"; a union of being and bliss — this is the higher Self.

He who thus understands, discerning the real from the unreal, ascertaining reality by his own awakened vision, knowing his own Self as partless awakening, freed from these things reaches peace in the Self.

Then melts the heart's knot of unwisdom without residue, when, through the ecstasy in which there is no doubt, arises the vision of the non-dual Self.

Through the mind's fault are built the thoughts of thou and I and this, in the supreme Self which is non-dual, and beyond which there is nothing; but when ecstasy is reached, all his doubts melt away through apprehension of the real.

Peaceful, controlled, possessing the supreme cessation, perfect in endurance, entering into lasting ecstasy, the ascetic makes the being of the All-self his own; thereby burning up perfectly the doubts that are born of the darkness of unwisdom, he dwells in bliss in the form of the Eternal, without deed or doubt.

They who rest on the Self that is consciousness, who have put away the outward, the imaginations of the ear and senses, and selfish personality, they, verily, are free from the bonds and snares of the world, but not they who only meditate on what others have seen.

The Self is divided by the division of its disguises; when the disguises are removed, the Self is lonely and pure; hence let the wise man work for the removal of the disguises by resting in the ecstasy that is free from doubt.

Attracted by the Self the man goes to the being of the Self by resting on it alone; the grub, thinking on the bee, builds up the nature of the bee.

The grub, throwing off attachment to other forms, and thinking intently on the bee, takes on the nature of the bee; even thus he who seeks for union, thinking intently on the reality of the supreme Self, perfectly enters that Self, resting on it alone.

Very subtle, as it were, is the reality of the supreme Self, nor can it be reached by gross vision; by the exceedingly subtle state of ecstasy it is to be known by those who are worthy, whose minds are altogether pure.   [360]

As gold purified in the furnace, rids itself of dross and reaches the quality of its own self, so the mind

ridding itself of the dross of substance, force and darkness, through meditation, enters into reality.

When purified by the power of uninterrupted intentness, the mind is thus melted in the Eternal, then ecstasy is purified of all doubt, and of itself enjoys the
essence of secondless bliss.

Through this ecstasy comes destruction of the knot
of accumulated mind-images, destruction of all works;
within and without, for ever and altogether, the form
of the Self becomes manifest, without any effort at all.

Let him know that thinking is a hundred times better
than scripture; that concentration, thinking the matter
out, is a hundred thousand times better than thinking;
that ecstasy free from doubt is endlessly better than
concentration.

Through unwavering ecstasy is clearly understood
the reality of the Eternal, fixed and sure. This cannot
be when other thoughts are confused with it, by the
motions of the mind.

Therefore with powers of sense controlled enter in
ecstasy into the hidden Self, with mind at peace perpetually; destroy the darkness made by beginningless
unwisdom, through the clear view of the oneness of the
real.

The first door of union is the checking of voice, the
cessation of grasping, freedom from expectation and
longing, the character bent ever on the one end.

A centering of the mind on the one end, is the cause
of the cessation of sensuality; control is the cause that
puts an end to imaginings; by peace, the mind-image
of the personality is melted away; from this arises un-

shaken enjoyment of the essence of bliss in the Eternal for ever, for him who seeks union; therefore the check-ing of the imagination is ever to be practiced effort-fully, O ascetic!

Hold voice in the self, hold the self in intellect, hold intellect in the witness of intellect, and, merging the witness in the perfect Self, enjoy supreme peace.

The seeker for union shares the nature of each dis-guise — body, vital breath, sense, mind, intellect — when his thoughts are fixed on that disguise.　　[370]

When he ceases from this sharing, the ascetic reaches perfect cessation and happiness, and is plunged in the essence of Being and Bliss.

Renouncing inwardly, renouncing outwardly — this is possible only for him who is free from passion; and he who is free from passion renounces all attachment within and without, through the longing for freedom.

Outward attachment arises through sensual objects; inward attachment, through personality. Only he who, resting in the Eternal, is free from passion, is able to give them up. Freedom from passion and awakening. are the wings of the spirit. O wise man, understand these two wings! For without them you cannot rise to the crown of the tree of life.

Soul-vision belongs to him who is free from passion; steady inspiration belongs to the soul-seer. Freedom from bondage belongs to the reality of inspiration; enjoyment of perpetual bliss belongs to the Self that is free.

.I see no engenderer of happiness greater than free-dom from passion for him who is self-controlled; if

very pure inspiration of the Self be joined to it, he
enters into the sovereignty of self-dominion. This is
the door of young freedom everlasting. There do thou
ever fix thy consciousness on the real self, in all ways
free from attachment to what is other than this, for
the sake of the better way.

Cut off all hope in sensual objects which are like
poison, the cause of death; abandon all fancies of birth
and family and social state; put all ritual actions far
away; renounce the illusion of self-dwelling in the body,
center the consciousness on the Self. Thou art the
seer, thou art the stainless, thou art in truth the supreme, secondless Eternal.

Firmly fixing the mind on the goal, the Eternal,
keeping the outward senses in their own place, with
form unmoved, heedless of the body's state, entering
into the oneness of Self and Eternal by assimilating the
Self and rising above all differences, for ever drink the
essence of the bliss of the Eternal in the Self. What
profit is there in other things that give no joy?   [378]

Firmly fix the mind
on the Goal

Free Even in Life

(Verses 379 — 438)

Ceasing to feed the imagination on things not Self, full of darkness, causing sorrow, bend the imagination on the Self, whose form is bliss, the cause of freedom.

This is the self luminous, witness of all, ever shining through the veil of the soul; making the one aim this Self, that is the contrary of all things unreal, realize it by identification with its partless nature.

Naming this from its undivided being, its freedom from all other tendency, let him know it clearly from being of the own nature of Self.

Firmly realizing self-hood in that, abandoning self-hood in the selfish personality, stand towards it as a disinterested onlooker stands towards the fragments of a broken vase.

Entering the purified inner organ into the witness whose nature is the Self, who is pure awakening, leading upward step by step to unmoving firmness, let him then gain vision of perfection.

Let him gain vision of the Self, freed from all disguises built up by ignorance of the Self — body, senses, vitality, emotion, personality — the Self whose nature is partless and perfect like universal ether.

The ether, freed from its hundred disguises — waterpots, jars, corn-measures and the like — is one and not divided, thus also the pure supreme, freed from personality, is one.

All disguises beginning with the Evolver and ending with a log are mirage only; therefore let him behold his own perfect Self, standing in the Self's oneness.

Whatever by error is built up as different from that, is in reality that only, not different from that. When the error is destroyed, the reality of the snake that was seen shines forth as the rope; thus the own-nature of all is the Self.

The Evolver is the Self, the Pervader is the Self, the Sky-lord is the Self, the Destroyer is the Self; all this universe is the Self; there is nothing but the Self.

Inward is the Self, outward also is the Self; the Self is to the east, the Self is also to the west. The Self is to the south, the Self is also to the north. The Self is above, the Self is beneath.

Just as wave and foam, eddy and bubble are in their own nature water; so, from the body to the personality, all is consciousness, the pure essence of consciousness. [390]

Being verily is all this world, that is known of voice and mind, there is nothing else than Being, standing on nature's other shore. Are cup and water-pot and jar anything but earth? He who is deluded by the wine of glamor speaks of "thou" and "I."

"When by repeated effort naught remains but this," the scripture says, declaring absence of duality, to put an end to false transference of reality.

Like the ether, free from darkness, free from wavering, free from limits, free from motion, free from change; having neither a within nor a without, having no other

than it, having no second, is the Self, the supreme
Eternal; what else is there to be known?

What more is there to be said? The Eternal, the
Life, the Self is seen here under many forms; all in this
world is the Eternal, the secondless Eternal; the scripture says "I am the Eternal"; knowing this clearly,
those whose minds are awakened, who have abandoned
the outward, becoming the Eternal, dwell in the Self,
which is extending consciousness and bliss. This, verily,
is sure.

Kill out desire that springs up through thought of
self in the body formed of darkness, then violent passion in the formal body woven of the breath. Knowing
the Self whose fame is sung in the hymns, who is eternal
and formed of bliss, stand in the being of the Eternal.

As long as the son of man enjoys this body of death,
he is impure; from the enemies arises the weariness
that dwells in birth and death and sickness. When he
knows the pure Self of benign form, immovable, then
he is free from these; — thus says the scripture too.

When all delusive qualities attributed to the Self are
put away, the Self is the supreme eternal, perfect, secondless, changeless.

When the activity of the imagination comes to rest
in the higher Self, the Eternal that wavers not, then no
more wavering is seen, and vain words only remain.

The belief in this world is built up of unreality. In
the one substance, changeless, formless, undifferentiated, what separateness can exist?

In the one substance, in which no difference of seer,
seeing, seen, exists, which is changeless, formless, un-

differentiated, what separateness can exist?   [400]

In the one substance, like the world-ocean full to overflowing, changeless, formless, undifferentiated, whence can separateness come?

Where the cause of delusion melts away, like darkness in light, in the secondless, supreme reality, undifferentiated, what separateness can there be?

In the supreme reality, the very Self of oneness, how could any word of difference dwell? By whom is difference perceived in purely blissful dreamlessness?

For this world no longer is, whether past, present, or to come, after awakening to the supreme reality, in the real Self, the Eternal, from all wavering free. The snake seen in the rope exists not, nor even a drop of water in the desert mirage, where the deer thirsts.

This duality is mere glamor, for the supreme reality is not twofold; thus the scripture says, and it is directly experienced in dreamlessness.

By the learned it has been perceived that the thing attributed has no existence apart from the substance, as in the case of the serpent and the rope. The distinction comes to life through delusion.

This distinction has its root in imagining; when imagining ceases it is no more. Therefore bring imagining to rest in the higher Self whose form is concealed.

In soul-vision the wise man perceives in his heart a certain wide-extending awakening, whose form is pure bliss, incomparable, the other shore, for ever free, where is no desire, limitless as the ether, partless, from wavering free, the perfect Eternal.

In soul-vision the wise man perceives in his heart

the reality free from growth and change, whose being is beyond perception, the essence of equalness, unequalled, immeasurable, perfectly taught by the words of inspiration, eternal, praised by us.

In soul-vision the wise man perceives in his heart the unfading, undying reality, which by its own being can know no setting, like the shimmering water of the ocean, bearing no name, where quality and change have sunk to rest, eternal, peaceful, one.　　　　　　[410]

Through intending the inner mind to it, gain vision of the Self, in its own form, the partless sovereignty. Sever thy bonds that are stained with the stain of life, and effortfully make thy manhood fruitful.

Standing in the Self, realize the Self in being, the Self from every disguise set free, Being, Consciousness, Bliss, the secondless; thus shalt thou build no more for going forth.

The mighty soul no more regards this body, cast aside like a corpse, seen to be but the shadow of the man, come into being as his reflection, through his entering into the result of his works.

Drawing near to the eternal, stainless awakening, whose nature is bliss, put very far away this disguise whose nature is inert and foul; nor let it be remembered again at all, for the remembrance of what has been cast forth builds for disdain. .

Burning this up with its root in the flame of the real Self, the unwavering Eternal, the wise man stands excellent as the Self, through the Self which is eternal, pure, awakening bliss.

The body is strung on the thread of works already

done, and is impure as the blood of slaughtered kine; whether it goes forward or stands, the knower of reality regards it not again, for his life is dissolved in the Eternal, the Self of bliss.

Knowing the partless bliss, the Self as his own self, with what desire or from what cause could the knower of reality cherish the body?

Of the perfect adept this is the fruit, of the seeker for union, free even in life — to taste without and within the essence of being and bliss in the Self.

The fruit of cleanness is awakening, the fruit of awakening is quiescence; from realizing the bliss of the Self comes peace, this fruit, verily, quiescence bears.

When the latter of these is absent, the former is fruitless. The supreme end is the incomparable enjoyment of the Self's bliss.   [420]

The famed fruit of wisdom is not to tremble before manifest misfortune. The various works that were done in the season of delusion, worthy of all blame — how could a man deign to do them after discernment has been gained?

Let the fruit of wisdom be cessation from unreality, a continuation therein is the fruit of unwisdom; — this is clearly seen. If there be not this difference between him who knows and him who knows not, as in the presence of the mirage to the thirsty deer, where is the manifest fruit of wisdom?

If the heart's knot of unwisdom be destroyed without remainder, how could sensual things cause continuance in unreality, in him who has no desire?

When mind-images arise not in the presence of sensual things, this is the limit of purity; when the personal idea does not arise, this is the limit of illumination. When life-activity that has been dissolved does not arise again, this is the limit of quiescence.

He whose thought is free from outward objects, through standing ever in the nature of the Eternal, who is as lightly concerned with the enjoyment of sensual things followed by others as a sleeping child, looking on this world as a land beheld in dream, when consciousness comes back, enjoying the fruit of endless holy deeds, he is rich and worthy of honor in the world.

This sage, standing firm in wisdom, reaches Being and Bliss, he is changeless, free from all acts, for his Self is dissolved in the Eternal.

Being that is plunged in the oneness of the Eternal and the Self made pure, that wavers not and is pure consciousness alone, is called wisdom.

They say he stands firm in wisdom, in whom this wisdom steadfastly dwells. He in whom wisdom is firmly established, who enjoys unbroken bliss, by whom the manifested world is almost unheeded, is called free even in life.

He who with thought dissolved is yet awake, though free from the bondage of waking life, whose illumination is free from impure mind-images, he, verily, is called free even in life.

He who perceives that his soul's pilgrimage is ended, who is free from disunion even while possessing division, whose imagination is free from imaginings, he, verily, is called free even in life.

He who even while this body exists, regards it as a

shadow, who has no sense of personality or possessions
— these are the marks of him who is free in life. [430]

Whose mind lingers not over the past, nor goes out
after the future, when perfect equanimity is gained,
this is the mark of him who is free even in life.

In this world, whose very nature is full of differences,
where quality and defect are distinguished, to regard
all things everywhere as the same, this is the mark of
him who is free even in life.

Accepting wished and unwished objects with equanimity in the Self, and changing not in either event, is
the mark of him who is free even in life.

When the sage's imagination is fixed on tasting the
essence of the bliss of the Eternal, so that he distin-
guishes not between what is within and without, this
is the mark of him who is free even in life.

Who is free from thought of "I" and "my," in body
and senses and their works, who stands in equanimity,
bears the mark of one who is free even in life.

He who has discerned the Eternal in the Self, through
the power of sacred books, who is free from the bondage of the world, bears the mark of one who is free
even in life.

He who never identifies himself with the body and
senses, nor separates himself in thought from what is
other than these, bears the mark of one who is free
even in life.   [438]

The Three Kinds of Works

(Verses 439 — 468)

H^E who through wisdom discerns that there is no division between the Eternal and the manifested world, bears the mark of one who is free even in life.

Whose mind is even, when honored by the good, or persecuted by the wicked, bears the mark of one who is free even in life.

In whom all sensuous objects, put forth by the supreme, melt together like the rivers and streams that enter the ocean's treasure house, making no change at all, since he and they are but the one Being, this sage self-conquered is set free.

For him who has understood the nature of the Eternal, there is no return to birth and death as of old; if such return there be, then the nature of the Eternal was not known.

If they say he returns to birth and death through the rush of old imaginings, this is not true; for, from the knowledge of oneness, imaginings lose all their power.

As the most lustful man ceases from desire before his mother; so, when the Eternal is known, the wise cease from desire, through fullness of bliss.

The scripture says that, even for him who profoundly meditates, there is a going after outward things of sense, on account of Works already entered on.

As long as there is the taste of pain and pleasure, so long are there Works already entered on; the fruits come from the acts that went before; without these acts where would the fruits be?

From the knowledge that I am the Eternal, the accumulated Works, heaped up even through hundreds of myriads of ages, melt away like the work of dream, on awaking.

Whatever one does while dreaming, however good or bad it seems, what effect has it on him, on awaking to send him either to hell or heaven?

On knowing the Self, unattached, enthroned like the 'dome of heaven, the man is no longer stained at all by Works to come.

As the ether enclosed in the jar is not stained by the smell of the wine, so the Self encompassed by its vestures, is not stained by any quality of theirs.   [450]

Works that have been entered on, before wisdom's sunrise, are not destroyed by wisdom, until they have reached their fruition; like an arrow aimed and sent forth at the mark.

The arrow discharged by the thought that there was a tiger, does not stop when it is seen to be a cow, but pierces the mark through its exceeding swiftness.

Verily, Works entered on are the most formidable to the wise, they disappear only through being experienced. But Works accumulated and Works to come both melt away in the fire of perfect wisdom.

When they have beheld the oneness of the Self and the Eternal, and stand ever firm in the power of that knowledge, for them those three kinds of Works exist no longer; for them there is only the Eternal, free from every change.

When the saint rests in the Self, through understanding that the Self is other than its vestures, that the Self is the pure Eternal; then the myth of the reality of Works entered on no longer holds him, just as the myth of union with things of dream no longer holds him who has awakened.

For he who is awake no longer keeps the sense of "I and mine and that," for his looking-glass body and the world that belongs to it; but comes to himself merely through waking.

Neither a desire for pursuing mythical objects, nor any-grasping after even a world full of them, is seen in him who has awakened. But if the pursuit of mirages goes on, then it is seen for certain that the man has not wakened from sleep.

Thus dwelling in the supreme Eternal, through the real Self, he stands and beholds naught else. Like the memory of an object looked on in dream, so is it, for the wise, with eating or the other acts of life.

The body is built up through Works; the Works entered upon make for the building up of various forms; but the Self is not built up through works.

"Unborn, eternal, immemorial," says the Scripture, whose words are not in vain; of him who rests in that Self, what building up of Works entered on can there be?

Works entered upon flourish then, when the Self is identified with the body; but the identifying of Self with body brings no joy, therefore let Works entered upon be renounced.   [460]

Even the building up of a body through Works en-

tered on is a mirage; whence can come the reality of a
mere reflected image? whence can come the birth of
an unreality?

Whence can come the death of what has not even
been born? Whence can come the entering on of what
does not even exist? — if there be a melting away of
the effects of unwisdom, root and all, through the
power of wisdom.

How does this body stand? In the case of him who
takes inert things to be real, Works entered on are sup-
ported by the sight of outward things — thus says the
scripture; yet it does not teach the reality of the body
and the like, to the wise.

One, verily, is the Eternal, without a second. There
is no difference at all. Altogether perfect, without beginning or end, measureless and without change.

The home of Being, the home of Consciousness, the
home of Bliss enduring, changeless; one, verily, without a second, is the Eternal. There is no difference
at all.

Full of the pure essence of the unmanifested, endless,
at the crown of all; one, verily, without a second, is
the Eternal; there is no difference at all.

That can neither be put away, nor sought after;
that can neither be taken nor approached — one, verily,
without a second, is the Eternal; there is no difference
at all.

Without qualities, without parts, subtle, without
wavering, without stain; one, verily, without a second,
is the Eternal; there is no difference at all.   [468]

Master and Pupil

(Verses 469 — 518)

THE TEACHER SPEAKS:

THAT, whose nature no man can define; where is no pasturage for mind or word; one, verily, without second, is the Eternal; there is no difference at all.

The fullness of Being, self-perfect, pure, awakened, unlike aught here; one, verily, without second, is the Eternal; there is no difference at all!

They who have cast away passion, who have cast away sensual delights, peaceful, well-ruled, the sages, the mighty, knowing reality in the supreme consummation, have gained the highest joy in union with the Self.

Thou worthy one also, seeking this higher reality of the Self, whose whole nature is the fullness of bliss, washing away the delusions thine own mind has built up, be free, gaining thy end, perfectly awakened.

Through Soul-vision, through the Self utterly unshaken, behold the Self's reality, by the clear eye of awakening; if the word of the scripture is perfectly perceived without wavering, then doubt arises no more.

On gaining freedom from the bonds bound by unwisdom as to the Self; in the gaining of that Self whose nature is truth, knowledge, bliss; the holy books, reason, and the word of the guide are one's evidences; an evidence too is the realizing of the Self, inwardly attained.

Freedom from bondage and joy, health of thought

and happiness, are to be known by one's self; the knowing of others is but inference.

As the teachers, who have reached the further shore, and the teachings tell, let a man cross over through that enlightenment which comes through the will of the higher Self.

Knowing the Self through one's own realization, as one's own partless Self, and being perfected, let him stand firm in the unwavering Self.

This is the last and final word of the teaching: The Eternal is the individual life and the whole world; rest in the partless One is freedom, in the Eternal, the secondless; and this too the scriptures show.

Through the word of the Guide, and the evidence of the teaching, understanding the highest Being, through union with the Self, he reached perfect peace, intent on the Self, so that nothing could disturb him any more, resting altogether in the Self.

Then after intending his mind for a while on the supreme Eternal, rising again from the highest bliss he spoke this word: [480]

The Pupil Speaks:

Entangling thought has fallen away, its activity has dissolved, through mastery of the Self's oneness with the Eternal; I know not this, nor anything that is not this; for what is it? how great is it? joy is its further shore.

This cannot be spoken by voice, nor thought by mind; I taste the glory of the ocean of the Supreme Eternal, filled full of the ambrosial bliss of the Self. My mind, enjoying delight, like a watercourse, that had dried up, when the multitude of waters come, is full of happiness, even from the slightest portion of the honey-sweet bliss of the Self.

Whither has this world of sorrow gone? what has taken it away? whither has it dissolved? Now I see that it no longer is — a mighty wonder!

What is there for me to reject? what to choose? what else exists? Where is there difference in the mighty ocean of the Eternal, full of the nectar of partless bliss?

I see not, nor hear, nor know aught of this world; for I bear the mark of the Self, whose form is being and bliss.

Honor, honor to thee, my Guide, mighty-souled; to thee, who art free from sensuous bondage, who art most excellent, whose own nature is the essence of bliss of the secondless Everlasting, whose words are ever a mighty, shoreless ocean of pity.

As one who was wearied with the heat, bathing himself and refreshed, in the enveloping light of the rayed moon, thus I have in a moment gained the partless excellent bliss, the imperishable word, the Self.

Rich am I, I have done what was to be done, freed am I from the grasp of the sorrowing world. My own being is everlasting bliss, I am filled full, through the favor of the Self.

Unbound am I, formless am I, without distinction am I, no longer able to be broken; in perfect peace am I, and endless; I am stainless, immemorial.

I am neither the doer nor enjoyer; mine are neither change nor act. I am in nature pure awakening. I am the lonely One, august for ever.   [490]

I am apart from the personal self that sees, hears, speaks, acts, and enjoys; everlasting, innermost, without act; the limitless, unbound, perfect Self awakened.

I am neither this nor that; I am even he who illumines both, the supreme, the pure; for me is neither inner nor outer, for I am the perfect, secondless Eternal.

The unequalled, beginningless reality is far from the thought of I and thou, of this and that; I am the one essence of everlasting bliss, the real, the secondless Eternal.

I am the Creator, I am he who makes an end of hell, he who makes an end of all things old; I am the Spirit, I am the Lord; I am partless awakening, the endless witness; for me there is no longer any Lord, no longer I nor mine.

For I, verily, consist in all beings, enveloping them within and without, through the Self that knows; I myself am at once the enjoyer and all that is to be enjoyed — whatever was seen before as separate — through identity with it.

In me, the ocean of partless Bliss, world-waves rise manifold, and fall again, through the storm-winds of glamor's magic.

In me, the material and other worlds are built up by glamor, through swift vibrations; just as in Time which has neither part nor division, are built up the world-periods, the years, the seasons, months, and days.

Nor does the Self, on which the worlds are built, become stained by them, even through the deluded who are stained by many sins; just as even a mighty flood of mirage waters wets not the salt desert earth.

Like the ether, I spread throughout the world; like the sun, I am marked by my shining; like the hills, I am everlasting and unmoved; I am like an ocean without shores.

I am not bound by the body, as the clear sky is not bound by clouds; whence then should the characters of waking, dreaming, dreamlessness, belong to me? [500]

The veil comes, and, verily, departs again; it alone performs works and enjoys them. It alone wastes away and dies, while I stand like a mighty mountain, forever unmoved.

Neither forth-going nor return belong to me, whose form is ever one, without division. He who is the one Self, without fissure or separation, perfect like the ether — how can he strive or act?

How should righteousness or sin belong to me, who possess not the powers of sense, who am above emotion, above form and change, who experience ever partless bliss; for the scripture teaches that in the Self is neither righteousness nor sin.

What is touched by his shadow, whether heat or cold, or foul or fair, touches not at all the man, who is other than his shadow.

The natures of things beheld touch not the beholder, who is apart from them, sitting above unchanged, as the character of the house affects not the lamp.

Like the sun which witnesses the act, like the tongued flame that leads the conflagration, like the rope that holds what is raised; thus am I, standing on the summit, the conscious Self.

I am neither the actor, nor the causer of acts; I am neither he who enjoys, nor he who brings enjoyment; I am neither the seer, nor he who gives sight; I am the unequalled Self, self-luminous.

When the disguise moves, just as the foolish-minded attribute to the sun the dancing of its reflection on the water, so one thinks: I am the doer, the enjoyer; I, also, am slain.

Let this inert body move on the waters or on dry land; I am not thereby stained by their natures, as the ether is not stained by the nature of a jar.

Acting, enjoying, baseness or madness, inertness or bondage or unloosing are the changes of the mind, and belong not really to the Self, the supreme Eternal, the pure, the secondless.   [510]

Let Nature suffer changes ten times, a hundred, a thousand times; what have I to do with these commotions?   For the lowering clouds touch not the sky.

From the unmanifest, down to grossest things, all this world encountered is a mere reflection only.   Like the ether, subtle, without beginning or end, is the secondless Eternal; and what that is, I am.

All-embracing, illumining all things; under all forms all-present, yet outside all; everlasting, pure, unmoved, unchanging, is the secondless Eternal; and what that is, I am.

Where the differences made by glamor have sunk to

final setting, of hidden nature, perceived in secret, the Real, Wisdom, Bliss, and formed of bliss, is the secondless Eternal; and what that is, I am.

Without act am I, without change, without division, without form; without wavering am I, everlasting am I, resting on naught else, and secondless.

I am altogether the Self, I am the All; I transcend all; there is none but me. I am pure, partless awakening; I too am unbroken bliss.

This sovereignty, self-rule, and mighty power, through the goodness of thy pity, power, and might, has been gained by me, my guide, great-souled; honor, honor to thee, and yet again honor.

In that great dream that glamor makes, in that forest of birth and age and death, I wander wearying; daily stricken by the heat, and haunted by the tiger of selfishness; thou hast saved me, my guide, by waking me out of sleep.   [518]

taste the essence of supreme bliss

The Perfect Sage

(Verses 519 — 548)

THE PUPIL SPEAKS:

HONOR to that one Being, wherever it is; honor to the Light which shines through the form of all that is; and to thee king of teachers!

Beholding him thus paying honor — a pupil full of worth, full of the joy of soul-vision, awakened to reality — that king of instructors, rejoicing in his heart, that mighty souled one, addressed to him this final word:

THE TEACHER SPEAKS:

This world is the offspring of the Eternal's thought; thus, verily, the Eternal is the Real in all things. Behold it thus by the vision of the higher Self, with mind full of peace, in every mode of being. A certain Being, apart from form, is seen everywhere, of those who have eyes to see. Therefore knowers of the Eternal understand that whatever is other than this, is but the sport and workmanship of intellect.

Who, being wise, and tasting that essence of supreme bliss, would delight any more in things of emptiness? Who desires to look on a painted moon, when the moon, the giver of delight, is shining?

For through enjoyment of unreal things, there is no contentment at all, nor any getting rid of pain. Therefore contented by enjoying the essence of secondless bliss, stand thou rejoicing, resting on the Self that is true Being.

Silence

Therefore beholding thyself everywhere, and considering thyself as secondless, let the time go by for thee, mighty minded one, rejoicing in the bliss that is thine own.

And wavering doubt in the Self of partless awakening which wavers not, is but of fancy's building; therefore through the Self which is formed of secondless bliss, entering into lasting peace, adore in silence.

In the silence is the highest peace, because wavering is the intellect's unreal work; there the knowers of the Eternal, mighty-souled, enjoy unbroken happiness of partless bliss, recognizing the Self as the Eternal.

There is no higher cause of joy than silence where no mind-pictures dwell; it belongs to him who has understood the Self's own being; who is full of the essence of the bliss of the Self.

Whether walking or standing, sitting or lying down, or wherever he may be, let the sage dwell according to his will, the wise man finding joy ever within himself.

No distinctions of place or time, position or space are to be regarded as bringing release from bondage, for the mighty-souled, who has perfectly attained to reality. Of what avail are the rites of religion for one who has attained to wisdom?

What religious rite will help one to know a jar, without having perceived it? But where there is direct perception, the object is perfectly understood.   [530]

So when there is direct perception, the Self shines forth clearly, without regard to place or time or rites of purification.

The direct knowledge, that "I am Devadatta," depends on nothing else; and it is precisely thus with the knowledge that "I am the Eternal," in the case of the knower of the Eternal.

How could the not Self, the mere chaff of unreality, be the illuminer of that through the radiance of which the whole world shines, as through the sun?

How can the scriptures or laws or traditions, or even all beings, illumine that by which alone they gain their worth?

This Self, self-illumined, is of unending power, immeasurable, the direct knowledge of all; knowing this, the knower of the Eternal, freed from bondage, most excellent, gains the victory.

Things of sense neither distress nor elate him beyond measure, nor is he attached to, or repelled by them; in the Self he ever joys, the Self is his rejoicing; altogether contented by the essence of uninterrupted bliss.

As a child, who is free from hunger and bodily pain, finds delight in play, so the wise man rejoices, free from the sorrow of "I" and "mine."

His food is what is freely offered, eaten without anxiety or sense of poverty; his drink is the pure water of the streams; he moves where fancy leads him, unconstrained; he sleeps by the river-bank, or in the wood; for his vesture is one that grows not old or worn; his home is space; his couch, the world; he moves in paths where the beaten road is ended; the wise man, delighting in the supreme Eternal.

Dwelling in this body as a mere temporary halting-place, he meets the things of sense just as they come, like a child subject to another's will; thus lives the knower of the Self, who shows no outward sign, nor is attached to external things.

Whether clothed in space alone, or wearing other vestures, or clothed in skins, or in a vesture of thought; like one in trance, or like a child, or like a shade, he walks the earth. [540]

Withdrawing desire from the things of desire, ever contented in the Self, the sage stands firm through the Self alone.

Now as a fool, now a wise man; now as a great and wealthy king; now a wanderer, now a sage; now dwelling like a serpent, solitary; now full of honor; now rejected and unknown; thus the sage walks, ever rejoicing in perfect bliss.

Though without wealth, contented ever; ever rejoicing, though without sensuous enjoyments; though not like others, yet ever seeming as the rest.

Ever active, though acting not at all; though tasting no experience, yet experiencing all; bodiless, though possessing a body; though limited, yet penetrating all.

This knower of the Eternal, ever bodiless, things pleasant or painful touch not at all, nor things fair or foul.

For pleasure and pain, things fair and foul, are for him who is bound by the vestures, who believes them real; but for him whose bonds are broken, for the sage whose Self is real Being, what fruit is fair, or what is foul?

Just as in an eclipse of the sun, people say, "the sun is darkened," though the sun indeed is not darkened, and they speak ignorantly, knowing not the truth of things.

Thus verily they behold the most excellent knower of Brahma as though bound to a body, while he is in truth freed for ever from the body, and they are deluded by the mere seeming of the body.   [548]

For Ever Free

THE SERPENT'S SLOUGH

BUT the body he has left, like the cast-off slough of a snake, remains there, moved hither and thither by every wind of life.

As a tree is carried down by a stream, and stranded on every shallow; so is his body carried along to one sensation after another.

Through the mind-pictures built up by works already entered on, the body of him who has reached freedom wanders among sensations, like an animal; but the adept himself dwells in silence, looking on, like the center of a wheel, having neither doubts nor desires.

He no longer engages his powers in things of sense, nor needs to disengage them; for he stands in the character of observer only. He no longer looks at all to the personal reward of his acts; for his heart is full of exultation, drunk with the abounding essence of bliss.

Leaving the path of things known or unknown, he stands in the Self alone; like a god in presence is this most excellent knower of the Eternal.

Though still in life, yet ever free; his last aim reached; the most excellent knower of the Eternal, when his disguise falls off, becoming the Eternal, enters into the secondless Eternal.

Like a mimic, who has worn the disguises of well-being and ill, the most excellent knower of the Eternal was Brahma all the time, and no other.

The body of the sage who has become the Eternal is consumed away, even before it has fallen to the ground — like a fresh leaf withered — by the fire of consciousness.

The sage who stands in the Eternal, the Self of being, ever full, of the secondless bliss of the Self, has none of the hopes fitted to time and space that make for the formation of a body of skin, and flesh, subject to dissolution.

Putting off the body is not Freedom, any more than putting away one's staff and waterpot; but getting free from the knots of unwisdom in the heart — that is Freedom, in very deed.

Whether its leaf fall in a running river, or on holy ground, prepared for sacred rites, what odds does it make to the tree for good or ill?

Like the loss of a leaf, or a flower, or a fruit, is the loss of the body, or powers, or vital breath, or mind; but the Self itself, ever one's own, formed of bliss, is like the tree and stands.

The divine saying declares the Self to be the assemblage of all consciousness; the real is the actor, and they speak only of the destruction of the disguise — unwisdom.

THE SELF ENDURES

(Verses 562 — 574)

Indestructible, verily, is the Self — thus says the scripture of the Self, declaring that it is not destroyed when all its changing vestures are destroyed.

Stones, and trees, grass, and corn, and straw are consumed by fire, but the earth itself remains the same. So the body, powers, life, breath and mind and all things visible, are burned up by the fire of wisdom, leaving the being of the higher Self alone.

As the darkness, that is its opposite, is melted away in the radiance of the sun, so, indeed, all things visible are melted away in the Eternal.

As, when the jar is broken, the space in it becomes clear space, so, when the disguises melt away, the Eternal stands as the Eternal and the Self.

As milk poured in milk, oil in oil, water in water, becomes perfectly one, so the sage who knows the Self becomes one with the Self.

Thus reaching bodiless purity, mere Being, partless, the being of the Eternal, the sage returns to this world no more.

He whose forms born of unwisdom are burnt up by knowledge of oneness with the everlasting Self, since he has become the Eternal, how could he, being the Eternal, come to birth again?

Both bonds and the getting rid of them are works of glamor, and exist not really in the Self; they are like the presence of the imagined serpent and its vanishing, in the rope which really does not change.

Binding and getting rid of bondage have to be spoken of, because of the existence, and yet the unreality, of enveloping by unwisdom. But there is no enveloping of the Eternal; it is not enveloped because nothing besides the Eternal exists to envelop it.

The binding and the getting rid of bondage are both mirages; the deluded attribute the work of thought to the thing itself; just as they attribute the cloud-born cutting off of vision to the sun; for the unchanging is secondless consciousness, free from every clinging stain.

The belief that bondage of the Real, is, and the belief that it has ceased, are both mere things of thought; not of the everlasting Real.

Therefore these two, glamor-built, bondage and the getting rid of bonds, exist not in the Real; the partless, changeless, peaceful; the unassailable, stainless; for what building-up could there be in the secondless, supreme reality, any more than in clear space?

There is no limiting, nor letting go, no binding nor gaining of success; there is neither the seeker of Freedom, nor the free; this, verily, is the ultimate truth.

BENEDICTION

(Verses 575 — 580)

This secret of secrets supreme, the perfect attainment, the perfection of the Self, has been shown to thee by me today; making thee as my new-born child, freed from the sin of the iron age, all thought of desire gone, making towards Freedom.

Thus hearing the teacher's words and paying him due reverence, he went forth, free from his bondage, with the Master's consent.

And he, the Teacher, his mind bathed in the happy streams of Being, went forth to make the whole world clean, incessantly.

Thus, by this Discourse of Teacher and Pupil, the

character of the Self is taught to those seeking Freedom, that they may be born to the joy of awakening.

Therefore let all those who put away and cast aside every sin of thought, who are sated with this world's joys, whose thoughts are full of peace, who delight in words of wisdom, who rule themselves, who long to be free, draw near to this teaching, which is dedicated to them.

To those who, on the road of birth and death, are sore stricken by the heat that the rays of the sun of pain pour down; who wander through this desert-world, in weariness and longing for water; this well-spring of wisdom, close at hand, is pointed out, to bring them joy — the secondless Eternal. This Teaching of Śankara's bringing Liberation, wins the victory for them.

Thus is ended THE CREST-JEWEL OF WISDOM, made by the ever-blessed ŚANKARA, pupil at the holy feet of GOVINDA his Teacher, the supreme Swan, the Wanderer of the World.

The Heritage of the Brâhmans

BY CHARLES JOHNSTON

The Heritage of the Brâhmans

IT is said that long ago, in the childhood of the world, the senses were so fine that we could hear the growing of the grass, the rustling of the opening buds of spring. By a memory of these early senses, by the faint remnant of them that the long ages in their passage have left us, we can hear now the faint stirring of the opening buds of a new spring of intellectual life, a new period in the spiritual thought of the world; and the key-note of this new period is the East, the wisdom of the East, the thought and ideals of the East.

Not merely or necessarily the East in latitude, but rather the Eastern side of man — that East in the soul of every man where the sun rises, where the light of intuition opens its first dawning rays, and, "rising, guides the lesser lives among its rays." And yet the East in latitude gives the key-note to the new dawn of thought in a special sense too. For it was in the East, and, more than all, in India, "mother of nations," that the eastern part of man where the sun rises found its best development; that the interior light of the soul found its fullest recognition.

And it is only natural that the minds of men, feeling the first gleam of dawning day, should turn towards the East; that they should grow enthusiastic for the Lands of the East, and, more than all, for India: that India should occupy an ever-widening space on the horizon of their thoughts; that their hearts should more and more turn towards India.

This growing interest and enthusiasm for India —
an enthusiasm at first almost instinctive, but gradually
quickened by advancing knowledge — is especially
felt today in the two most idealistic nations in the
West, the Americans and the Germans. For with all
their sense of practical life and practical development,
the Americans and Germans are at heart idealists;
ready to sacrifice all their practical aims and practical
accomplishment to a vision; ready, as Emerson said,
to leave Cleopatra and the army, to seek the sources
of the Nile.

The deepest curiosity of the Americans and Germans,
turning towards India, unquestionably centers on the
Brâhmans; one hears again and again the words — the
wisdom of the Brâhmans, the ideal of the Brâhmans,
the life of the Brâhmans; and the first question one is
always asked refers to the Brâhman order. To answer
this question, it would be necessary to write many vol-
umes; to trace the rise of the Brâhman order in the
dim twilight of Vedic days; to show the growth and con-
solidation of their power in the days of Râma, and
through the struggles of the great war of the Pạ̄ndu
and Kuru princes; to point to certain dark sides of their
development that had become visible in Buddha's days;
and at last to fill in the splendid picture of Brâhmanic
advance and Brâhmanic development in Śankarâchârya's days.

When the records of the monasteries of Southern
India are more fully known and understood, when the
Smârta Brâhmans who have preserved most clearly the
splendid tradition of Śankara relax a little their reserve,

we shall — it can hardly be doubted — have a picture of that great man and his times as perfect and full of color as the picture we have of Plato's times, and the thought of Plato who, more than any other philosopher, resembles Śankara.

What we know of Śankara already, though only a tithe of what we may know when old records are opened, is enough to give him a place amongst the choicest spiritual aristocracy of the world, as a seer and thinker who towered above his race as Plato towered above the Greeks; as a Great Man, an elder brother of the race, whose thought and insight mark a high tide of human life.

There is a dim tradition, in the oldest Indian books, in the great Upanishads, and the earlier Vedic hymns, that the Brâhmans were not in the beginning the spiritual teachers of India; that they received their earliest wisdom from the Royal Sages of the Râjanya or Kshattriya race. But the Brâhmans have so long held these treasures of wisdom as their own— guarding them as a mother her child, as a man his first-born — that they have come to consider them as their very own; their heritage rather by birth than by adoption. The fact that, in spite of this jealous love of their darling treasures, they have preserved the tradition of their earliest Royal Teachers, points to the most valued feature in the Brâhmans' character; — the unflinching, unalterable fidelity with which they have preserved, unaltered and inviolate, the spiritual treasures committed to their care; and the safe-guarding of which through the ages forms their truest and greatest title of fame;

the best justification for that instinctive turning towards the Brâhmans as the center and representative of Indian genius, which we have noted as so marked a feature of the Indian Renaissance today.

But once the Brâhmans had received the wisdom-doctrines from their Royal Teachers, their distinctive genius, their most valued quality, began to assert itself. With their unparalleled genius for order, their instinctive feeling for preservation, they recorded, classified and developed the intuitive wisdom of the Royal Sages — Buddha, a Royal Sage of far later days, has put on record this unparalleled fidelity: "those ancient Rishis of the Brâhmans, versed in the Three Wisdoms, the authors of the verses, the utterers of the verses, whose ancient form of words so chanted, uttered, or composed, the Brâhmans of today chant over again and repeat; intoning or reciting, exactly as has been intoned or recited." — *(Tevigga Sutta)*.

That Krishṇa, the spiritual hero of the Mahâbhârata war, whose mission it was to usher in the Iron Age of Kali Yuga, was no Brâhman but a Kshattriya, who traced his doctrines from Manu the Kshattriya through the Royal Sages, is enough to show that in the days of the great war, the Brâhmans had not yet claimed as quite their own the teachings of wisdom which it was their mission to hand down through the ages. *(Bhagavad-Gîtâ, iv)*.

The great war, according to Indian tradition, was fought out five thousand years ago. And, after the great war, in which so many Kshattriya princes fell, the keeping of the Sacred records began to pass completely into the hands of the Brâhmans. The Brâhmans, sensible of their great mission, prepared themselves to carry it out by forming a high ideal of life; by strict rules of conduct and discipline which only the highest characters could support; and the very strictness of which seems to have produced a reaction which we see traces of in Buddha's days.

The life of the Brâhman was conceived and moulded in accordance with his high ideal; in accordance with his high destiny as transmitter of the wisdom of the Golden Age across the centuries to our dark iron days. Purity, unworldliness, and discipline were the key-notes of his life; and the Brâhman's unparalleled genius for order gradually moulded this ideal into a set of definite rules, a series of religious ceremonies, which laid hold on his life before he saw the light of day, and did not loose that hold when his body vanished among the red embers of the funeral pyre — but rather kept in touch with him, through the Śraddha offering to the shades for nine generations after his death.

This life of ceremonies and rites, the key-note of which was the acquiring and transmission of the Three Wisdoms spoken of by Buddha, gradually made of the Brâhman order a treasure-box or casket for the safer keeping of the holy records handed down. Whether the Brâhmans were originally of the fair, almost white race which forms their nucleus today, and whose distinctive physical character and color make a Brâhman of pure type at once recognizable in an assemblage of Hindus, is a question difficult to solve. We find in the oldest Indian books that: "The color of the Brâhman is white," and this, in later days became a sentence symbolical of their ideal of purity; but in the beginning it may have been a description of their color, an index of their race.

It is very probable that this fair, almost white race, which now forms the nucleus of the Brâhman order, gradually became, through selective genius, through their unequalled instinct of order, the recognized repository and transmitter of the sacred records of the past. But the ideal life of the Brâhman was, perhaps, too arduous for the common lot of man; at any rate we see a gradually increasing tendency to degeneration in one side of the Brâhman's life; for in India as in other lands, even silver clouds have their dark linings.

Their instinct for order, among the Brâhmans of lesser moral structure than the high ideal of their race, became an instinct for ceremonial; their ideal of purity became a habit of outward purification; and they tended to harden into an exclusive priestly caste, withdrawn from, and above the common life of man. The priestcraft, by a second step, began to weave ambitions, to seek a share of political power, and at last, a practical predominance in the state, which threatened to become a spiritual tyranny.

But these developments, inseparable from the weakness of human life, were but the rusting of the outer layer of the casket in which the wisdom of the Golden Age was handed down. There were also within the Brâhman order — as there are today — men who held to the high ideal of their past; who were fitting repositories of the high tradition they were destined to carry down. The casket in which were held the records of the past had always its lining of precious metal, though the outside might rust and tarnish with the passing ages.

The greatest of these followers of that high idea, in later days, within the Brâhman caste, was Sankarâchârya, the Brâhman Sage of Southern India. It is hard to say, with certainty, when Sankara lived; but the records of Sringiri, where his successors have held rule over the nucleus of the Brâhman order, point to a period about two millenniums ago; a period, that is, just outside the threshold of our era.

Sankarâchârya began the work of reforming the Brâhman caste from within. A few centuries before him, Buddha had scattered broadcast through India, and Buddha's followers had scattered broadcast through the world, the teachings of India's Golden Days, in a form readily intelligible for all, and to be assimilated by the simplest mind of man.

It remained to do for India, what, perhaps, others were doing, across the Himalayas, for the whole world; to preserve inviolate, and transmit in its purity that other side of wisdom which the simplest heart of man can intuitively feel; but which only the most perfectly developed powers, the most fully expanded intellect and spiritual insight can fully and consciously grasp; it remained to secure the preservation of those profounder truths and that deeper knowledge which only the finest powers of the soul can adequately comprehend.

To secure their preservation in India was the duty

and mission of Śankarâchârya. Believing that this preservation should be helped and seconded by whatever aids selective race genius and hereditary capacity could give, he confined the transmission of this wisdom, and of the records which contained it, entirely within the Brâhman order, as far as our knowledge goes. There is evidence that, among the Brâhmans of Southern India in early days, were a certain number of families not belonging to that white race which forms the nucleus of the Brâhman caste; but belonging to the dark, almost black Dravidian peoples of Southern India, who are the survivors, perhaps, of a land that once lay to the south of India, but has now vanished beneath the waves. This dark Dravidian race has produced many men of remarkable genius and power, whose insight and force quite fitted them for inclusion in the Brâhman order.

But as the centuries moved on, such admission became more difficult; till, in the days of Śankara, it is probable that the door was completely closed. What changes Śankara made in the Brâhman order which followed him, in the division of the Brâhmans which recognized his transcendent force, can only be known with surety to the Brâhmans of that order themselves. But this much we know, that Śankara did all his overpowering genius could accomplish to turn the Brâhmans from too exclusive following after ceremonial; to lead them back to the spiritual wisdom, the recognition of the inner light of the soul, which was India's greatest heritage; and that, taking India's most precious records, the Great Upanishads, he rendered them into the thought and language of his own day, and did all that a marvelous insight and a literary style of wonderful lucidity could do to make the spirit and the genius of the Upanishads live once more in the hearts of the Brâhmans of his time.

He set himself, above all, to cleanse the inner lining of the casket where India's treasures lay concealed; to remove every speck from the precious metal whose perfect purity alone could guarantee the costly contents against rust and moth. The reforms inaugurated by Sankarâchârya continue to bear fruit today; the new light he shed on the old records, the new insight he gave to the old symbols, are the treasured inheritance of the Smârta Brâhmans, whose spiritual heads, in unbroken succession, have ruled at Sringiri Math, in the mountains of Northern India.

Centuries passed, and the sunlit plains of India were filled with Moslem invaders, falling like swarms of locusts on the rich gardens of that distant wonderland; full of the fierce hostility of fanaticism against the symbols of a religion they did not understand; and against the Brâhmans, as ministers of this religion. It would not be wonderful, it would rather be perfectly natural, if this hostility and predominance of a foreign fanatical power had sealed the lips of the Brâhmans once for all as to the mysteries of their religion; had locked and double-locked the casket in which the heritage of India lay concealed.

But in spite of tyranny and fanaticism that would have justified the most perfect reticence, the most absolute silence, the Brâhmans retained an ideal of their

universal mission, above and beyond their mission to
their own land and their own religion. No sooner did
brighter days dawn for them under the Emperor Akbar,
the great Indian monarch of the sixteenth century who
conceived and framed a high ideal of religious toler-
ance and mutual understanding which was the nearest
approach to State Theosophy; no sooner did the
brighter day dawn than the Brâhmans were ready to
forget old griefs and to teach their Moslem rulers the
broad principles of their religion.

Two generations after Akbar, Akbar's noblest and
most ill-fated descendant, Prince Dara Shukoh, received
from the Brâhmans the permission to translate into
Persian a series of the Upanishads, including the Great
Upanishads of which something has been already said.
This Persian translation, besides following the words
of the old records, put into visible form much that had
been hidden between the lines, and followed, in some degree, the new light that had been shed on the Upanishads by the genius of Śankarâchârya.

This Persian translation of the Upanishads, which
embodies a very valuable tradition of their hidden
meaning, made about the year 1640, was found by Anquetil Duperron in 1775, and by him translated into
Latin. From Anquetil Duperron this "Key to the Indian Sanctuary" passed to Schopenhauer, and becoming "the comfort of his life, the comfort of his death"
led him to prophesy that Indian Renaissance which is
glowing with the fair colors of dawn today.

But under Dara Shukoh's brother, the fanatical
Aurungzeb, darker days fell upon the Brâhmans; and

they suffered much from European nations more presumptuous and not less fanatical than Aurungzeb; of these the darkest record clings to the Portuguese, who tried to wring from the Brâhmans the heart of their mystery by Inquisition and *auto-da-fé*.

Yet, once more, just a hundred years ago when a group of Europeans full of love for the East, sought from the Brâhmans some knowledge of their learning, the Brâhmans, with singular generosity, made these Europeans in some degree sharers in their heritage. From the knowledge thus freely given to these Europeans, whose chiefs were William Jones and Thomas Colebrooke, the first foundations of Orientalism were laid; and a field of matchless fertility was opened to a growing band of workers who enrolled themselves under the banner of the East.

But the last and finest insight, the master-key to the records was still treasured in the East itself; somewhat of that insight has since been freely offered to us; on our ability to use it most probably depends the further insight that the future holds in promise.

The Awakening to the Self

ÂTMA BODHA

The Awakening to the Self

THIS awakening to the Self is recorded for those whose inner darkness has been worn away by strong effort, who has reached restfulness, from whom passion has departed, who seek perfect Freedom.

Among all causes, wisdom is the only cause of perfect Freedom; as cookery without fire, so perfect Freedom cannot be accomplished without wisdom.

Works cannot destroy unwisdom, as these two are not contraries; but wisdom destroys unwisdom, as light the host of darkness.

At first wrapped in unwisdom, when unwisdom is destroyed the pure Self shines forth of itself, like the radiant sun when the clouds have passed.

When life that was darkened by unwisdom is made clear by the coming of wisdom, unwisdom sinks away of itself, as when water is cleared by astringent juice.

This world is like a dream, crowded with loves and hates; in its own time it shines like a reality; but on awakening it becomes unreal.

This passing world shines as real, like the silver imagined in a pearl-shell, as long as the Eternal is not known, the secondless substance of all.

In the real conscious Self, the all-penetrating everlasting pervader, all manifested things exist, as all bracelets exist in gold.

Just like the ether, the Lord of the senses, the Radiant, clothed in many vestures, seems divided because these are divided, but is beheld as one when the vestures are destroyed.

Through this difference of vesture, race, name, and home are attributed to the Self, as difference of taste and color to pure water.

Built up of fivefold-mingled elements through accumulated works is the physical vesture, the place where pleasure and pain are tasted.

Holding the five life-breaths, mind, reason, and the ten perceiving and acting powers, formed of unmingled elements, is the subtle vesture, the instrument of enjoyment.

Formed through the beginningless, ineffable error of separateness, is the causal vesture. One should hold the Self to be different from these three vestures.

In the presence of the five veils, the pure Self seems to share their nature; like a crystal in the presence of blue tissues.

The pure Self within should be wisely discerned from the veils that surround it, as rice by winnowing, from husk and chaff.

Though ever all-present, the Self is not everywhere clearly beheld; let it shine forth in pure reason like a reflection in a pure mirror.

The thought of difference arises through the vestures, the powers, mind, reason, and nature; but one must find the Self, the witness of all this being, the perpetual king.

Through the busy activity of the powers, the Self seems busy; as the moon seems to course through the coursing clouds.

The vestures, powers, mind, and reason move in their paths under the pure consciousness of the Self, as people move in the sunshine.

The qualities of vestures, powers, and works are attributed to the spotless Self through undiscernment, as blue to the pure sky.

Through unwisdom, the mental vesture's actorship is attributed to the Self, as the ripple of the waves to the moon reflected in a lake.

Passion, desire, pleasure, pain move the mind; but when the mind rests in deep sleep they cease; they belong to the mind, not to the Self.

Shining is the sun's nature; coldness, the water's; heat, the fire's; so the Self's nature is Being, Consciousness, Bliss, perpetual spotlessness.

The Self lends Being and Consciousness, and mind lends activity. When these two factors are joined together by undiscernment, there arises the feeling that 'I perceive.'

The Self never changes; and mind of itself cannot perceive; but the Self through error believes itself to be the habitual doer and perceiver.

The Self is believed to be the habitual life, as a rope is believed to be a snake; and thus fear arises. But when it is known that 'I am not the habitual life but the Self' then there can be no more fear.

The Self alone lights up the mind and powers, as a flame lights up a jar. The Self can never be lit by these dull powers.

In the knowledge of the Self, there is no need that

it should be known by anything else. A light does not need another light; it shines of itself.

Putting all veils aside, saying 'it is not this! it is not this!' one must find the real unity of the habitual Self and the Supreme Self, according to the words of wisdom.

All outward things, the vestures and the rest, spring from unwisdom; they are fugitive as bubbles. One must find the changeless, spotless 'I am the Eternal.'

As I am other than these vestures, not mine are their birth, weariness, suffering, dissolution. I am not bound by sensuous objects, for Self is separate from the powers of sense.

As I am other than mind, not mine are pain, rage, hate, and fear. The Self is above the outward life and mind, according to the words of wisdom.

From this Self come forth the outward life and mind, and all the powers; from the Self come ether, air, fire, the waters, and earth upholder of all.

Without quality or activity, everlasting, free from doubt, stainless, changeless, formless, ever free am I the spotless Self.

Like ether, outside and inside all, I am unmoved; always all-equal, pure, unstained, spotless, unchanged.

The ever-pure lonely one, the partless bliss, the secondless, truth, wisdom, endless, the Supreme Eternal; this am I.

Thus the steadily-held remembrance that 'I am the Eternal' takes away all unwisdom, as the healing essence stills all pain.

In solitude, passionless, with powers well-ruled, let

him be intent on the one, the Self, with no thought but that endless one.

The wise through meditation immersing all outward things in the Self, should be intent on that only Self, spotless as shining ether.

Setting aside name, color, form, the insubstantial causes of separateness, the knower of the supreme rests in perfect Consciousness and Bliss.

The difference between knower, knowing, and known exists not in the Self; for through its own Consciousness and Bliss it shines self-luminous.

Thus setting the fire-stick of thought in the socket of the Self, let the kindled flame of knowledge burn away the fuel of unwisdom.

By knowledge, as by dawn, the former darkness is driven away; then is manifest the Self, self-shining like the radiant sun.

Yet the Self, though eternally possessed, is as though not possessed, through unwisdom. When unwisdom disappears, the Self shines forth like a jewel on one's own throat.

Separate life is conceived in the Eternal by error, as a man is imagined in a post. But the pain of separation ceases when the truth about it is perceived.

By entering into real nature, wisdom swiftly arises. Then the unwisdom of 'I' and 'mine' disappears, as when a mistake about the position of north and south is set right.

The seeker after union, possessed of all knowledge, sees with the eye of wisdom that all things rest in the Self; and this Self is the One, the All.

Self is all this moving world; other than Self is naught. As all jars are earth, so he beholds all as the Self.

Perfect Freedom even in life is this, that a man should shake himself free from all the limits of his disguises, through the essence of Reality, Consciousness, Bliss, just as the grub becomes the bee.

Crossing the ocean of glamor, and slaying the monsters, passion and hate, the seeker for union, perfect in peace, grows luminous in the garden of the Self.

Free from bondage to outward, unlasting pleasures, and returning to the joy of the Self, he shines pure within like the flame in a lamp.

Even when hidden under disguises, let the Sage stand free from them, like pure ether. Though knowing all, let him be as though he knew nothing; moving untrammelled like the air.

Let the Sage, shaking off his disguises, merge himself utterly in the all-pervading One; as water in water, ether in ether, flame in flame.

The gain above all gains, the joy above all joys, the wisdom above all wisdoms; let him affirm that it is the Eternal.

When this is seen, there is no more to see; when this is attained, there is no more to attain; when this is known, there is no more to know; — let him affirm that this is the Eternal.

Upward, downward, on all sides perfect; Being, Consciousness, Bliss; the secondless, endless, everlasting One; — let him affirm that this is the Eternal.

Through the knowledge that nothing is but the Eter-

nal, the unchanging One is beheld by the wise; the
aboriginal, partless joy; let him affirm that this is the
Eternal.

As partakers in the bliss of that partless, blissful
One, the Evolver and all the powers enjoy their bliss
as dependents.

Every being is bound to the Eternal; every movement
follows the Eternal; the all-embracing Eternal is in all,
as curd is in all milk.

Nor small nor great nor short nor long, nor born nor
departing, without form, attribute, color, name; — let
him affirm that this is the Eternal.

Through whose shining shine the sun and all lights;
but who shines not by any's light; through whom all
this shines; — let him affirm that this is the Eternal.

All present within and without, making luminous all
this moving, the Eternal shines forth glowing of red-
hot iron.

The Eternal is different from the moving world —
yet other than the Eternal is naught! What is other
than the Eternal shines insubstantial, like the mirage
in the desert.

Things seen and heard are not other than the Eternal. Knowledge of reality teaches that all this is the
Eternal, the Being, Consciousness, Bliss, the secondless.

The eye of wisdom beholds the ever-present Consciousness, Bliss, the Self, the eye of unwisdom beholds
not, as the blind beholds not the shining sun.

The personal life, refined through and through by
the fire of wisdom, which right learning and knowledge
kindle, shines pure as gold, freed from every stain.

The Self, rising in the firmament of the heart — sun of wisdom, darkness-dispersing, all-present, all-supporting — shines forth and illumines all.

He who, drawing away from space and time, faithfully worships in the holy place of the divine Self — the ever-present, the destroyer of heat and cold and every limit, the stainless, eternally happy — he all-knowing, entering the All, becomes immortal.

(Thus the Awakening to the Self is completed.)

The Awakening to Reality

TATTVA BODHA

Śankara's Catechism

INTRODUCTORY BY CHARLES JOHNSTON

IN the "Awakening to the Self," and, still more, in the "Crest Jewel of Wisdom," Śankara the Teacher uses many words in a clear, precise, and consciously exact sense, which is not always to be gathered from the context of these two works. In the "Awakening to the Self," this is hardly an impediment, as the expression of this excellent poem is so perfect and universal; nor is there any great impediment in the first part of the "Crest Jewel of Wisdom," which has been translated under the title "First Steps on the Path." But further on in the "Crest Jewel," this is not the case. It becomes more strict and technical in meaning; and without precise definitions, much is hardly intelligible. But in the "Crest Jewel" itself these definitions are not always to be found. What is to be done then, if we really want to understand the Teacher precisely?

Happily Śankara has left us a Key in his own work, the "Awakening to Reality," where nearly every special word of his philosophy is exactly defined. We have only to try to find the best English translation of his definitions, and we shall have a clear clue and outline to the larger work, the "Crest Jewel," and, indeed, to the whole of Śankara's philosophy.

One thing must be remembered. This "Awakening to Reality" is what we have called it — a catechism. And in a catechism we can hardly expect the perfect poetical form and splendid imagery of works like the "Awakening to the Self." What we shall find, is lucidity, accuracy, grasp, coherence; but not poetical beauty. Thus is begun:

THE AWAKENING TO REALITY

I

To the Master, the World-Soul, the Master of seekers for union, obeisance; to the teacher, the giver of wisdom. To fulfill love for those who would be free, this Awakening to Reality is addressed to them.

THE FOUR PERFECTIONS

We shall tell of the way of discerning reality, the perfection of freedom, for those who are fitted by possessing the Four Perfections.

What are the Four Perfections?

— The Discerning between lasting and unlasting things; No Rage for enjoying the fruit of works, either here or there; the Six Graces that follow Peace; and then the Longing to be free.

What is the Discerning between lasting and unlasting things?

— The one lasting thing is the Eternal; all, apart from it, is unlasting.

What is No Rage?

— A lack of longing for enjoyments here and in the heaven-world.

What is possession of the Perfections that follow Peace?

— Peace; Self-Control; Steadiness; Sturdiness; Confidence; Intentness.

What is Peace?

— A firm hold on emotion.

What is Self-Control?

— A firm hold on the lust of the eyes and the outward powers.

What is Steadiness?

— A following out of one's own genius.

What is Sturdiness?

— A readiness to bear opposing forces, like cold and heat, pleasure and pain.

What is Confidence?

— Confidence is a reliance on the Voice of the Teacher and Final Wisdom.

What is Intentness?

— One-pointedness of the imagination.

What is the Longing to be free?

— It is the longing: "That Freedom may be mine."

THE DISCERNING OF REALITY

These are the Four Perfections. Through these, men are fitted to discern Reality.

What is the Discerning of Reality?

— It is this: the Self is real; other than it, all is fancy.

SELF, VESTURES, VEILS, MODES

What is the Self?

— He who stands apart from the Physical, the Emotional, and the Causal Vestures; who is beyond the five

Veils; who is witness of the three Modes; whose own nature is Being, Consciousness, Bliss — this is the Self.

THE THREE VESTURES

What is the Physical Vesture?

— Being formed of the five creatures fivefolded, born through works, it is the house where opposing forces like pleasure and pain are enjoyed; having these six accidents: it is, is born, grows, turns the corner, declines, perishes; such is the Physical Vesture.

What is the Emotional Vesture?

— Being formed of the five creatures not fivefolded, born through works, the perfection of the enjoyment of opposing forces like pleasure and pain, existing with its seventeen phases: the five powers of knowing; the five powers of doing; the five lives; emotion, one; the soul, one; this' is the Emotional Vesture.

The five powers of knowing are: Hearing, Touch, Sight, Taste, Smell. Hearing's radiation is Space; Touch's, Air; Sight's, the Sun; Smell's, the Twin Physicians; these are the powers of knowing.

Hearing's business is the seizing of sounds; Touch's business, the seizing of contacts; Sight's business, the seizing of forms; Taste's business, the seizing of tastes; Smell's business, the seizing of odors.

The five powers of doing are: Voice, Hands, Feet, Putting-forth, Generating. Voice's radiation is the Tongue of Flame; Hands', the Master; Feet's, the Pervader; Putting-forth's, Death; Generating's, the Lord of Beings; thus the radiations of the powers of doing.

Voice's business is speaking; Hands' business is grasping things; Feet's business is going; Putting-forth's business is removing waste; Generating's business is physical enjoying.

What is the Causal Vesture?

— Being formed through ineffable, beginningless unwisdom, it is the Substance and Cause of the two Vestures; though unknowing as to its own nature, it is yet in nature unerring; this is the Causal Vesture.

THE THREE MODES

What are the Three Modes?

— The Modes of Waking, Dreaming, Dreamlessness.

What is the Mode, Waking?

— It is where knowledge comes through Hearing and the other knowing powers, whose business is sound and the other perceptions; this is the Waking Mode.

When attributing itself to the Physical Vesture, the Self is called the Pervading.

Then what is the Mode, Dreaming?

— The world that presents itself in rest, generated by impressions of what has been seen and heard in the Mode, Waking, is the Mode, Dreaming.

When attributing itself to the Emotional Vesture, the Self is called the Radiant.

What then is the Mode, Dreamlessness?

— The sense that I perceive outwardly nothing at all, that rest is joyfully enjoyed by me, this is the Mode, Dreamlessness.

When attributing itself to the Causal Vesture, the Self is called the Intuitional.

THE FIVE VEILS

What are the Five Veils?

— The Food-formed; the Life-formed; the Emotion-formed; the Knowledge-formed; the Bliss-formed.

What is the Food-formed?

— Coming into being through the essence of food, getting its growth through the essence of food, in the food-formed world it is again dispersed, this is the Food-formed Veil — the Physical Vesture.

What is the Life-formed?

— The Forward-life and the four other Lives, Voice and the four other powers of doing; these are the Life-formed.

What is the Emotion-formed Veil?

— Emotion, joining itself to the five powers of knowing — this is the Emotion-formed Veil.

What is the Knowledge-formed?

— The Soul, joining itself to the five powers of knowing — this is the Knowledge-formed Veil.

What is the Bliss-formed?

— This verily is the Substance not quite pure because of the unwisdom that gives birth to the Causal Vesture; in it are founded all joys; this is the Bliss-formed Veil.

Thus the Five Veils.

By saying: "Mine are the lives; mine is emotion; mine is the soul; mine is the wisdom"; these are recognized as possessions. And just as a bracelet, a necklace, a house and such things separated from one's self, are recognized as possessions, so the Five Veils and the Vestures, recognized as possessions, are not the Self (the Possessor).

What then, is the Self?

— It is that whose own-nature is Being, Consciousness, Bliss.

What is Being?

— What stands through the Three Times (Present, Past, Future) — this is Being.

What is Consciousness?

— The own-nature of Perceiving.

What is Bliss?

— The own-nature of Joy.

Thus let a man know that the own-nature of his own Self is Being, Consciousness, Bliss.

EXPLANATORY BY CHARLES JOHNSTON

This "Awakening to Reality" is a summary of an intuition of the world, a solution of the universe. Only those who have certain mental and moral endowments are ripe for the understanding of such a solution of the world. Briefly, these endowments are: wisdom and will. The solution reached is — the real Self of every man is the Eternal. This Self is inwardly beginningless, endless, immortal. But outwardly it becomes manifest as three lesser selves, each with its own vesture, its own world.

Lowest of these is the physical self, the "Pervading"; with its physical Vesture, in the Waking world.

Next, the emotional self, the "Radiant," with its emotional Vesture, in the Dreaming world.

Highest, the causal self, the "Intuitional," with its causal Vesture, in the Dreamless world. It has existence apart from the Eternal, owing only to the thin veil of illusion, which hides the identity of the One with the All. Thus, as to its own nature, it is unknowing; for, while believing itself One, it is really All. But for all other things it is unerring, for its close proximity to, and real oneness with, the Eternal, give it the inner sense of the trueness of things that is all wisdom. This is "the Seer who ordained all fitly through the ages."

In the Physical Vesture adheres one Veil; in the Emotional Vesture three — the vital, the emotional, the moral; — in the Causal, again one.

There is a great difficulty in finding a fit word for the term we have translated "radiation." What is meant is the power — personified, almost personal — conceived to be the "regent" or "deity" of the field in which each mode of perception and action finds its expansion. A closely analogous phrase would be, for instance, "the Prince of the Powers of the Air," who would thus be the "regent" or "deity" of the powers of touch, and, in morals, the "lusts of the flesh."

This is, of course, mythology: a mythical representation of an actual truth, very difficult to represent otherwise than mythologically.

But in the conclusion of the matter there is no difficulty. It is, that a man shall know the own-nature of his own Self to be Being, Consciousness, Bliss; or, in other words, Eternal, Wisdom, Love.

II

We shall speak now of the way the four-and-twenty natures are developed.

THE PRIMITIVE SEVEN

Dwelling together with the Evolver in glamor, who is the very self of the three potencies: substance, force, and space.
From this glamor, shining ether came forth.
From shining ether, breath came forth.
From breath, fire came forth.
From fire, the waters came forth.
From the waters, earth came forth.

THEIR SUBSTANTIAL PARTS

Now, among these five natures:
From the substantial part of shining ether, the power of hearing came forth.
From the substantial part of breath, the power of touch came forth.
From the substantial part of fire, the power of seeing came forth.
From the substantial part of the waters, the power of taste came forth.
From the substantial part of earth, the power of smelling came forth.
From the united substantial parts of these five natures, the inner powers — mind, soul, self-assertion, imagination — came forth.

Mind is the very self of intending and doubting.
Soul is the very self of affirmation.
Self-assertion is the very self of attributing selfhood.
Imagination is the very self of image-making.

The regent of mind is the Moon.
The regent of soul is the Evolver.
The regent of self-assertion is the Transformer.
The regent of imagination is the Pervader.

THEIR FORCEFUL PARTS

Now, among these five natures:
From the forceful part of shining ether, the power of voice came forth.
From the forceful part of breath, the power of handling came forth.
From the forceful part of fire, the power of moving came forth.
From the forceful part of the waters, the power of engendering came forth.
From the forceful part of earth, the power of extruding came forth.
From the united forceful parts of these natures, the five lives — the upward-life, the forward-life, the uniting-life, the distributing-life, the downward-life — came forth.

THEIR SPATIAL PARTS

Of these five natures, from their spatial parts, the five-folded five elements come forth.
What is this five-folding?
It is this: taking the spatial parts of the five primi-

tive natures — one part of each — these parts are each first divided in two; then one half of each part is left alone, on one side, while the other halves of each are each divided into four. Then to the half of each nature, is joined the fourth of the half [the eighth] of each of the other natures. And thus five-folding is made.

From these five primitive natures, thus five-folded, the physical vesture is formed. Hence the essential unity between the clod and the Evolving Egg.

THE LIFE AND THE LORD

There is an image of the Eternal, which attributes itself to the vestures, and is called the Life. And this Life, through the power of Nature, regards the Lord as separate from itself.

When wearing the disguise of Unwisdom, the Self is called the Life.

When wearing the disguise of Glamor, the Self is called the Lord.

Thus, through the difference of their disguises, there is an appearance of difference between the Life and the Lord. And as long as this appearance of difference continues, so long will the revolving world of birth and death continue. For this reason the idea of the difference between the Life and the Lord is not to be admitted.

But how can the idea of unity between the self-assertive, little-knowing Life, and the selfless, all-knowing Lord, be accepted, according to the famous words, *that thou art;* since the genius of these two, the Life and the Lord, is so opposite?

This is not really so; for 'Life attributing itself to the physical and emotional vestures' is only the verbal meaning of *thou;* while the real meaning of *thou* is 'pure Consciousness, bare of all disguises, in dreamless life.'

And so 'the Lord full of omniscience and power' is but the verbal meaning of *that;* while the real meaning of *that* is 'pure Consciousness stripped of disguises.'

Thus there is no contradiction in the unity of the Life and the Lord, since both are pure Consciousness.

THE FREE-IN-LIFE

And thus all beings in whom the idea of the eternal has been developed, through the words of wisdom and the true Teacher, are Free-in-life.

Who is Free-in-life?

Just as there is the firm belief that 'I am the body,' 'I am a man,' 'I am a priest,' 'I am a serf,' so he who possesses the firm conviction that 'I am neither priest nor serf nor man, but stainless Being, Consciousness, Bliss, the Shining, the inner Master, Shining Wisdom,' and knows this by direct perception, he is Free-in-life.

THE THREE MODES OF DEEDS

Thus by the direct knowledge that 'I am the Eternal,' he is freed from all the bonds of his deeds.

How many modes of these 'deeds' are there? If counted as 'deeds to come,' 'deeds accumulated,' and 'deeds entered on,' there are three modes.

The pure and impure deeds that are done by the body

of the wise, after wisdom is won, are called 'deeds to come.'

And what of 'deeds accumulated'? The deeds that are waiting to be done, sprung from seeds sown in endless myriads of births, are 'deeds accumulated.'

And what are 'deeds entered on'? The deeds that give joy and sorrow here in the world, in this vesture, are 'deeds entered on.' Through experiencing them they reach cessation; for the using-up of deeds entered on comes through experiencing them. And 'deeds accumulated' reach cessation through wisdom, the very self of certainty that 'I am the Eternal.' 'Deeds to come' also reach cessation through wisdom. For, as water is not bound to the lotus-leaf, so 'deeds to come' are not bound to the wise.

For those who praise and love and honor the wise, to them come the pure 'deeds to come' of the wise. And those who blame and hate and attack the wise, to them come all the unspeakable deeds, whose very self is impurity, of the wise man's 'deeds to come.'

THE END

Then the Knower of the Self, crossing over the circling world, even here enjoys the bliss of the Eternal. As the sacred books say: The Knower of the Self crosses over sorrow.

And the sacred traditions say: Whether he leave his mortal form in Benares or in a dog-keeper's hut, if he has gained wisdom, he is free, his limitations laid aside.

Thus the Awakening to Reality is completed.

Śankara's Catechism

EXPLANATORY BY CHARLES JOHNSTON

IN THE first part of Śankara's Catechism, previously translated, the most valuable thing is the teaching of the sevenfold man, who is really a modified unity appearing in seven modes. The only real and eternal element in the sevenfold man — for real and eternal are, for Śankara, synonymous terms — is the perfect Self, which is one with the Eternal. In manifestation this Self appears in three degrees: the intuitional self, the emotional self, the physical self; and, for each of these there is a vesture suited to its nature. Thus the divine Self, with its three degrees, and their three vestures, make up the perfect seven.

The three lesser degrees of the Self are its representatives in the three manifest worlds: the spiritual world, the middle world, the physical world. And, very naturally, the middle world partakes in some degree of the nature of the other two; so that its highest layer is touched with the nature of the spiritual world, while its lowest layer is touched with the nature of the physical world.

This threefold nature of the middle world finds its counterpart in the three veils which make up the vesture of the middle self, which we have called the emotional self as perhaps the best description of its total nature.

The three veils of the middle self are the vital veil,

the sensuous veil, and the intellectual veil; and the regents of the last two are 'mind' and 'soul,' as we have translated the original terms — Manas and Buddhi.

Development takes place, therefore, by the gradually raising of the self through these vestures and veils; so that, having begun as the physical self in pure animal life, it gradually becomes the emotional and intellectual self of human life, then the intuitional self of life that is something more than human, and at last realizes itself as the eternal Self which is one with the Eternal.

To this, the first part of the Catechism, is then added the outline of Śankara's idealistic physics, the doctrine of the three potencies of substance, force, space; or, as one might call it, from a different point of view, the three modes of subject, predicate, object: of the knower, the knowing, the known. And as perception is of five types, the subject, predicate, and object are divided into the five types of sensuous perception. But as the objects of sensuous perception are not simple, but each respond to several different sensations, a description is found for this fact in the 'process of five-folding' of the object. As an example, a piece of camphor responds not only to the sense of sight but to other senses, touch, taste, smell; it is therefore conceived as made up of the five natures that are objects of sensuous perception, so mingled that one nature is dominant. The three potencies and the five natures are the three vestures and the five veils, from another point of view.

Very important are the definitions: 'mind' is the power of intending and doubting; 'soul' is the power of affirmation; the latter approaching the intuitional self which is the 'enlightened spiritual will.' To express in terms of morals this psychological analysis, we may say that at first through the power of self-assertion, the idea of selfhood is falsely attributed to the physical body and its animal nature, and then to the mental picture of the physical body, which is the emotional self or lower personality. The task of regeneration, of initiating true life, consists in first checking this false self-assertion — selfishness and sensuality — and then through the stages of 'intending and doubting' and strong 'affirmation' substituting for the lower personality the enlightened spiritual will, which is the direct expression of the real Self, re-becoming the Eternal.

Then this chapter of physics and psychology is followed by one of metaphysics. There is the real Self, which is the Eternal. But we do not realize our life as that real Self. Why do we not realize it? Because of two errors, or illusions, which make up the double 'heresy of separateness.' The first error is the error of our apartness from the Eternal. The second error is the error of our apartness from each other. The removal of these two errors constitutes 'our duty towards God' and 'our duty towards our neighbor'; in both cases the real gain is our own, is the gain of our real Self.

Śankara calls the first error glamor; the second, unwisdom. The picture of the self formed through the first is the Lord; the picture of the self formed through the second is the Life. And the real nature of both is the same — pure consciousness — though there is a verbal difference, a difference of definition, between them.

Then, in conclusion, the three forms of 'deeds' or Karma. We may compare 'accumulated deeds' to capital; 'deeds entered on,' to interest; and 'deeds to come,' to the earnings of an unselfish man for the good of others. And we must remember that each of these has a debit as well as a credit side.

The real value of this little treatise is as a key and outline of longer and more complicated works; yet it has a high excellence of its own.

The Essence of the Teaching

VÂKYA SUDHÂ, OR BÂLA BODHANÎ

The Essence of the Teaching

SEER AND SEEN

THE form is seen, the eye is seer; the mind is both seen and seer. The changing moods of mind are seen, but the witnessing Self, the seer, is never seen.

The eye, remaining one, beholds varying forms; as, blue and yellow, coarse and fine, short and long; and differences such as these.

The mind, remaining one, forms definite intentions, even while the character of the eye varies, as in blindness, dullness, or keen-sightedness; and this holds also of hearing and touch.

The conscious Self, remaining one, shines on all the moods of mind: on desire, determination, doubt, faith, unfaith, firmness and the lack of it, shame, insight, fear, and such as these.

This conscious Self rises not, nor has its setting, nor does it come to wax or wane; unhelped, it shines itself, and illumines others also.   [5]

THE PERSONAL IDEA

This illumining comes when the ray of consciousness enters the thinking mind; and the thinking mind itself is of twofold nature. The one part of it is the personal idea; the other part is mental action.

The ray of consciousness and the personal idea are blended together, like the heat and the hot iron ball. As the personal idea identifies itself with the body, it brings that also a sense of consciousness.

The personal idea is blended with the ray of consciousness, the body, and the witnessing Self, respectively — through the action of innate necessity, of works, and of delusion.

Since the two are bound up together, the innate blending of the personal idea with the ray of consciousness never ceases; but its blending with the body ceases, when the works wear out; and with the witnessing Self, through illumination.

When the personal idea melts away in deep sleep, the body also loses its sense of consciousness. The personal idea is only half expanded in dream, while in waking it is complete.   [10]

The power of mental action, when the ray of consciousness has entered into union with it, builds up mind-images in the dream-state; and external objects, in the waking state.

The personal form, thus brought into being by the personal idea and mental action, is of itself quite lifeless. It appears in the three modes of consciousness; it is born, and so also dies.

THE POWERS OF GLAMOR

For the world-glamor has two powers — extension and limitation, or enveloping. The power of extension brings into manifestation the whole world, from the personal form to the universal cosmos.

This manifesting is an attributing of name and form to the Reality — which is Being, Consciousness, Bliss, the Eternal; it is like foam on the water.

The inner division between the seer and the seen, and the outer division between the Eternal and the world, are concealed by the other power, limitation; and this also is the cause of the cycle of birth and death. [15]

The light of the witnessing Self is united with the personal form; from this entering in of the ray of consciousness arises the habitual life — the ordinary self.

The isolated existence of the ordinary self is attributed to the witnessing Self, and appears to belong to it; but when the power of limitation is destroyed, and the difference appears, the sense of isolation in the Self vanishes away.

It is the same power which conceals the difference between the Eternal and the visible world; and, by its power, the Eternal appears subject to change.

But when this power of limitation is destroyed, the difference between the Eternal and the visible world becomes clear; change belongs to the visible world, and by no means to the Eternal.

The five elements of existence are these: being, shining, enjoying, form and name; the three first belong to the nature of the Eternal; the last two, to the nature of the visible world.   [20]

In the elements — ether, air, fire, water, earth; in creatures — gods, animals, and men, Being, Consciousness, Bliss are undivided; the division is only of name and form.

Six Steps of Soul Vision

Therefore setting aside this division through name and form, and concentrating himself on Being, Consciousness, Bliss, which are undivided, let him follow after soul-vision perpetually, first inwardly in the heart, and then in outward things also.

Soul-vision is either fluctuating or unwavering; this is its two-fold division in the heart. Fluctuating soul-vision is again two-fold; it may consist either in things seen or heard.

This is the fluctuating soul-vision which consists in things seen: a meditating on consciousness as being merely the witness of the desires and passions that fill the mind.

This is the fluctuating soul-vision which consists in things heard: the constant thought that "I am the self, which is unattached, Being, Consciousness, Bliss, self-shining, secondless." [25]

The forgetting of all images and words, through entering into the bliss of direct experience — this is un-wavering soul-vision, like a lamp set in a windless place.

Then, corresponding to the first, there is the soul-vision which strips off name and form from the element of pure Being, in everything whatever; now accomplished outwardly, as it was before, in the heart.

And, corresponding to the second is the soul-vision which consists in the unbroken thought, that the Real is a single undivided Essence, whose character is Being, Consciousness, Bliss.

Corresponding to the former third, is that steady being, is the tasting of this Essence for oneself. Let him fill the time by following out these, the six stages of soul-vision.

When the false conceit, that the body is the Self, falls away; when the Self supreme is known; then, whithersoever the mind is directed, there will the powers of soul-vision arise. [30]

The knot of the heart is loosed; all doubts are cut;

all bondage to works wither away — when That is known, which is the first and the last.

THE THREE SELVES

The individual self appears in three degrees: as a limitation of the Self; as a ray of the conscious Self; and, thirdly, as the self imagined in dreams. The first alone is real.

For the limitation in the individual self is a mere imagination; and that which is supposed to be limited is the Reality. The idea of isolation in the individual self is only an error; but its identity with the Eternal is its real nature.

And that song they sang of "That thou art" is for the first of these three selves alone; it only is one with the perfect Eternal, not the other selves.

The power of world-glamor, existing in the Eternal, has two potencies: extension and limitation. Through the power of limitation, Glamor hides the undivided nature of the Eternal, and so builds up the images of the individual self and the world.   [35]

The individual self which comes into being when the ray of consciousness enters the thinking mind, is the self that gains experience and performs works. The whole world, with all its elements and beings, is the object of its experience.

These two, the individual self and its world, were before time began; they last till Freedom comes, making up our habitual life. Hence they are called the habitual self and world.

In this ray of consciousness, the dream-power exists,

with its two potencies of extension and limitation. Through the power of limitation, it hides the former self and world, and so builds up a new self and a new world.

As this new self and world are real only so long as their appearance lasts, they are called the imaginary self and the imaginary world. For, when one has awakened from the dream, the dream existence never comes back again.

The imaginary self believes its imaginary world to be real; but the habitual self knows that world to be only mythical, as also is the imaginary self.

The habitual self looks on its habitual world as real; but the real Self knows that the habitual world is only mythical, as also is the habitual self.

The real Self knows its real oneness with the Eternal; it sees nothing but the Eternal, yet sees that what seemed the unreal is also the Self.

Freedom and Final Peace

As the sweetness, the flowing, and the coldness, that are the characteristics of the water, reappear in the wave, and so in the foam that crests the wave;

So, verily, the Being, Consciousness, and Bliss of the witnessing Self enter into the habitual self that is bound up with it; and, by the door of the habitual self, enter into the imaginary self also.

But when the foam melts away, its flowing, sweetness, coldness, all sink back into the wave; and when the wave itself comes to rest, they sink back to the sea.

When the imaginary self melts away, its Being, Consciousness, Bliss sink back into the habitual self; and, when the habitual self comes to rest, they return to the Self supreme, the witness of all.

The Teachings of Śankara

BY CHARLES JOHNSTON

The Teachings of Śankara

TRADITION, our best guide in many of the dark problems of India's past, attributes the admirable philosophical work we have just translated to Śankarâchârya, the greatest name in the history of Indian Philosophy, and one of the greatest masters of pure thought the world has ever seen.

Śankara, again according to the tradition of the East, lived and taught some two thousand years ago, founding three colleges of Sanskrit learning and philosophy, the most important being at Śringeri, in southern India. He wrote Commentaries on the older Vedânta books, and many original works of great excellence, of which this is reckoned to be one.

Like all Śankara's separate works, *The Essence of the Teaching* is complete in itself, containing a survey of the whole of life, from a single standpoint; in the present case, from the point of view of pure intellect.

The moral problem before us, is the liberation of our souls from the idea of personality; and the opening of the door to the life of the universal Self, which will enter our hearts, and rule them, once the personal idea is put out of the way. And there is no more potent weapon for combating the personal idea than the clear and lucid understanding that what we call our personality is, in reality, only one of many pictures in the mind, a picture of the body, held before our consciousness, viewed by it, and therefore external to it. If the personality is a picture in the field of consciousness, it cannot be consciousness itself; cannot be our real self; but must necessarily be unreal and transient.

We are the ray of consciousness, and not the image of the body which it lights up, and which, thus lit up, we call our personality. And here we come to one point of the highest interest, in the present work: its central ideas anticipate, almost in the same words, the most original teachings of German philosophy. Hence a right understanding of it will bridge over one of the chasms between the East and the West, the remote past and the life of today; thus showing, once more, that the mind of man is everywhere the same; that there is but one Soul making itself manifest throughout all history.

It may be enough, here, to point out that German philosophy — the teaching of Kant, as developed by Schopenhauer — regards each individual as a manifestation of the universal Will, a ray of that Will, fallen into manifestation, under the influence of the tendency called the will-towards-life.

This individualized ray of the universal Will, falling into the intellect, becomes thereby subject to the powers which make for manifestation, and which Kant analyzed as Causality, Time, and Space. For Kant has shown, with admirable cogency and lucidity, that these so solid-seeming realities are not real at all, but were forms of our thought; mere figments of our intellects. What we call manifestation, Schopenhauer calls representation; and he has very fully developed the idea of the Universe as the resultant of the universal Will, manifested through these three forms of representation — Causality, Time, and Space.

Now it is quite clear that he calls Universal Will what

Śankara, following the Upanishads, calls the Eternal; and that the forms of representation of Schopenhauer's system, correspond to the World-glamor, or Mâyâ, of Indian thought. And it is further clear that the will-toward-life, or desire for sensuous existence, of the one system, is very close to the personal idea, or egotism, of the other.

Whoever is acquainted with the two systems, can point out a further series of analogies; we shall content ourselves with alluding to one. Schopenhauer taught that our salvation lies in denying the personal and selfish will-toward-life, within ourselves, and allowing the Universal Will to supersede it; — the very teaching which lies at the heart of Indian thought: the supersession of the individual self by the Self universal, the Self of all beings.

To turn now from the purely intellectual, to the moral side of the matter. If we consider it well, and watch the working of the powers of life we find within us, we shall see that all our misery and futility come from this very source, the personal idea — the vanity and selfishness of our own personalities, coming into strife with the equally vain and selfish personalities of others.

There is not an evil that cannot be traced to this fertile source. Sensuality, for example, with all its attendant crime and pain, is built on two forces, both springing from the personal idea: first, the desire for the stimulus of strong sensation, to keep the sense of the separate, isolated self keen and vivid; and then the vanity and foolish admiration of our personal selves, as possessors of such abundant means of gratification. Another evil, the lust of possessions, is of the same brood;

and, curiously enough, the root of it is — fear; the cow-
ering fear of the personal self, before the menacing forces
of the world; the desperate, and — infallible accompani-
ment of cowardice — remorselessly cruel determination
to build up a triple rampart of possessions between the
personality and the mutability of things. The whole
cause of the race for wealth, the cursed hunger for gold,
is a fearful and poltroon longing for security, protection
for the personal self; which, indeed, as a mere web of
dreams and fancies, is in very bad need of protection.

The last evil, ambition, which is only vanity grown
up, is so manifestly of the same color with the others
that no special indication of the fact is needed. Thus
we see what an immense part of human life, and that,
the most futile and pitiable part of it, is built up on so
slight a foundation: the wholly mythical personality,
the web of dreams, the mere image of a body, itself
unreal, which has usurped a sort of sovereignty over
all the powers of our wills and minds.

The whole problem for us is this, and it is one that
recurs in every moment of life: to disperse this web of
dreams which we call our personality, and so to let the
pure and universal Will pour into our hearts, to follow
out its own excellent purposes, and manifest its own
beneficent powers. And thus we shall for the first time
enter into our inheritance; no longer as shadowy and
malevolent sprites, raging between earth and heaven, a
sorrow to the angels, a mockery to the fiends; but rather
as undivided parts of the great soul of humanity; of
that universal Self, whose own nature is perfect Being,
perfect Consciousness, perfect Bliss.

The Song of the Self

SIDDHÂNTA-TATTVA-VINDU

The Song of the Self

Nor earth nor water, fire nor liquid air,
  Nor ether, nor the powers, nor these in one;
Undifferentiated, in dreamless perfect rest,
That, the One, final, blest, alone, am I.

Nor castes nor their divisions, rite nor rule,
Are mine, nor fixing mind and thought and mood;
No longer dreaming things not Self art 'I' and 'mine,'
That, the One, final, blest, alone, am I.

Nor mother, father, nor the gods and worlds,
Nor Scriptures, offerings, shrines are there, they say,
In dreamlessness abandoned by the lonely Self;
That, the One, final, blest, alone, am I.

Nor sectary of Cause or Lord or Life
Knows That, nor follower of Saint or Rite,
In perfect union, pure of all but Self,
That, the One, final, blest, alone, am I.

Nor upward, downward, nor within, without;
Nor midward, backward, That, nor east nor west;
All-present everywhere in partless unity,
That, the One, final, blest, alone, am I.

Nor white nor black nor yellow, That, nor red;
Nor small nor very great nor short nor long;
Formless, yet like a light, a star;
That, the One, final, blest, alone, am I.

Nor teacher, teaching, learner, what is learned;
Nor thou nor I nor this expanded world;
Conscious of its own form, from error free,
That, the One, final, blest, alone, am I.

Nor waking, mine, nor dream, nor dreamless sleep;
Nor fire of life or heart or seeing soul;
These three are of unwisdom; but the fourth,
That, the One, final, blest, alone, am I.

Even expanded for the sake of Self —
Self, that, still perfect, on no other rests —
All the wide world besides is little worth.
That, the One, final, blest, alone, am I.

Nor is this first with any second to it;
Nor lonely this, nor yet has it compeers;
Nor is this secondless One void or filled with aught;
How shall I tell this perfect wisdom's crowd?

Appendix

Appendix

Prepared for presentation by the Theosophical Club in the Temple of Peace at Point Loma. (Adapted from many sources)

I LOVE to think of those great beings, those royal-hearted Ones, who return to earth to shed their divine compassion in order to lift the veil into those inner realms of light for those who are ready to look within. Could we not recount among ourselves here tonight some of the strange legendary tales that have been woven about the life of Śankarâchârya, who lived from 510 B. C. to 478 B. C.? For all that mystic lore is a magic tapestry woven of Truth itself.

Have you ever heard of the portents that attended Śankara's birth? It is said that the whole celestial host gave forth paeans of gladness. With no selfish or partial joy, but for the sake of religion they rejoiced, because creation, engulfed in the ocean of pain, was now to obtain perfect release.

The mountains themselves were swayed by the wind of his perfect merit. On every hand the world was greatly shaken, as the wind drives the tossing boat; so also the minutest atoms of sandal perfume, and the hidden sweetness of precious lilies floated on the air, and rose through space, and then commingling, came back to earth; so again the garments of Devas descending from heaven touching the body, caused delightful thrills of joy; the sun and moon with constant course redoubled the brilliancy of their light, whilst in the world the fire's gleam of itself prevailed without the use of fuel. Pure water flowed from springs self-caused, and rare and special flowers in great abundance bloomed out of season.

And more marvelous still, whatever wealth was requisite, there did it appear upon earth. From the midst of the pure snowy mountains a wild herd of white elephants came of themselves without noise, not curbed by any, self-subdued, and every kind of colored horse, in shape and quality surpassingly excellent, with sparkling jewelled manes and flowing tails, came prancing 'round, as if with wings.

Among men enmity and envy gave way to peace. Content and rest prevailed on every side; whilst there was closer union amongst the true of heart. Discord and variance were entirely appeased, and all possessed themselves in harmony.

Who was this babe that heaven and earth should thus give forth their bounty? Were not similar tales told of the childhood of the great Buddha? And have we not also been taught that Buddha and Śankarâchârya are most closely connected? Both were Avatâras of a high mystical order, though not belonging to the same class of these superior Beings.

But to return to the marvelous boy himself. It is said that in his first year he acquired the Sanskrit alphabet and his own language. At the age of two he learned to read. At three he studied the Purânas and understood many portions of them by intuition. And in his seventh year, having attained all that his preceptor could teach him, he returned home.

Nor was he lacking in occult powers at an early age. Once when his mother lay in a swoon, as he stood beside her he drew the river that flowed on the hither side of the field up out of its bed, that its pure waters might refresh her.

Kings and others of high birth and intellect sought him even at this early age that he might teach them of secret wisdom never uttered except in guarded places.

Do you know the tale of how he gained his mother's consent to letting him become a holy ascetic? It runs in this wise: She with her mother's pride in his lofty attainments of soul and mind, could not endure the idea that he should shut himself away from the beauties and pleasures of life, and firm was she in her refusal of his request. But the young Śankara could sometimes act with the wile of a young and clever god. So going down to the river one day to bathe he soon was alarming his mother by his cries for help. She ran to the river's brink and saw that a great alligator held the boy's foot in a deadly grip. In helpless agony she stood by the edge of the stream. Then said the boy, "The beast has imparted to me that if you will grant my request and let me become a holy ascetic, he will loosen his hold." Whereupon the mother gave her consent, and the alligator with great tranquillity opened its jaws and released the youth, who clambered out of the river and lost no time in preparing to leave his home, giving over his mother into the care of friends and relatives, and telling her he would come back to her whenever she should need his presence.

There was living at this time in a cave in the hillside near the Nerbudda River a sage, Govind Yati by name. Years ago Vyâsa had appeared to him telling of the coming of a youth who would demonstrate the most miraculous powers. And so it came to pass. When Śankara left his mother he traveled for many days through forests, over hills, by towns and across rivers, led by an irresistible force, he knew not what. After a time he found himself at the opening of the cave in the hillside where dwelt the sage Govind Yati. Straightway he became the pupil of the wise man and was taught the four great truths of Brahma, namely: *Knowledge is Brahma, the soul is Brahma, Thou art That,* and *I am Brahma.* Then one day as Govind Yati was immersed in contemplation a furious tempest arose. Violent thunder shook the heavens, the ethereal vault was riven with tongues of lightning; rain deluged the earth, and Śankara, without awaking his master, quelled the storm, as quietly as a child is soothed by the sound of sweet music. And when the sage returned to consciousness and learned of what had befallen, he was filled with great joy and said: "Thus has the prophecy of Vyâsa been fulfilled."

Then the sage blessed Śankara, and knowing that the youth's sojourn with him had come to an end, bestowed his benediction upon him and bade him proceed to the holy city of Benares that he might there receive the blessing of the Deity. "Go," said he, "on thy glorious work, then enter, and begin to save mankind!"

Thus admonished, Śankara turned his steps to Benares, and here it was that he received his first pupil, Sanandana, the same who afterwards became celebrated as his greatest favorite under the title of Padmapada, he for whom the enlightened youth reserved his greatest powers of instruction.

Is there not a tale connected with the acquiring of the name Padmapada by this dear pupil?

The chroniclers of old tell the story thus: There were among Śankara's disciples some within whom envy was aroused at witnessing the unusual attachment that existed between the youthful sage and his cherished pupil. Śankara wished to dispel these envious feelings and show them that it was through superior merit alone that Sanandana was chosen among them for higher instruction and closer communion with the Teacher. So standing one day on the banks of the river which ran near his dwelling-place, he called to Sanandana who stood on the other side among his companions, to come over to him directly. Sanandana forthwith without any hesitation and with dauntless spirit stepped upon the flowing waters of the river and moved towards his Teacher with stedfast and graceful mien. And lo! At each step a lovely lotus sprang from the bosom of the waters, trailing a starry line of blossoms behind him as he stepped lightly upon the bank. Then said Śankarâchârya, as he embraced Sanandana: "Henceforth shall you be known among us as Padmapada, 'He of the Lotus-path.' "

But tarry a moment. Have we not run ahead of our story? It was many years ere this, indeed when he was but twelve years of age that he made his dwelling upon the banks of the Ganges and there wrote the great works that men who seek wisdom have studied ever since: his Commentaries on the Sûtras, the Upanishads, and on the *Bhagavad-Gîtâ*. In later years when Padmapada came to him bewailing the loss of one of his precious Commentaries which as it chanced had been destroyed by his uncle, Śankara without any perturbation recited the contents of that which had been destroyed in the exact words familiar to all his pupils while Padmapada rewrote them as he spoke.

Nor did such feats as this mark the limit of his mental powers. He was so wise and so well versed in the vast learning of the Vedas, that his name was sounded as victor in all philosophical discussions and debates. Once he went to the city of Mahishmati where dwelt the sage Mandana Misra. He was led towards the house of this wise man by a number of parrots miraculously endowed with human speech, who, so the story runs, discoursed upon weighty philosophical questions. But when he reached the door of the dwelling he found it fast shut. Undismayed he arose in the air and entered from above, alighting just beside Mandana Misra in his spacious hall. Then began an animated discussion between the astonished host and his unexpected guest. The sun rose high in the heavens and found them deep in their debate; it sloped down the sky in its westering course and yet the two, each of redoubtable intellect, continued. At length as evening crept upon them they called on the wife of Mandana Misra to act as umpire between them; but she, busy housewife that she was, deemed it not thrifty to let the hours pass attending to the discourse of word-spinners, so with ready wit she brought two garlands of fresh flowers saying: "Wear these as you talk, and he whose garland does not wither shall be deemed victor." So the two each put on his garland and in no long time Mandana Misra's was limp and faded like the leaves of a delicate tree beneath the rays of the summer sun. But Sankara's remained fresh as when first brought in at dewy eve.

And that is but the beginning of the story, for the victor claimed his opponent as a disciple. And the wife — she we learn was none other than Sarasvatî in corporeal form. Nor would Sankarâchârya be content until he had held debate with her. Many were the questions put to him by his fair adversary, but always was he to the fore with a ready answer. Then Sarasvatî, for so we may now call her, turned into a path of thought to which Sankara was an utter stranger. She asked him a question on the science of love! For the first time no answer was forthcoming, yet even such a question must be solved by the sage. So he left Mandana Misra's city in search of an answer. He traveled for some time with his disciples and came at length to a forest.

Now it so happened that a certain king named Amaraka lay dying here at the foot of a tree surrounded by many friends mourning his departure. As the soul of the dying man took flight an unusual thing happened. Śankara left his own body, entrusting it to the care of his disciples. He entered that of the dead king, and the monarch's followers, seeing their chief rise once again with the light of life in his eyes, were overjoyed beyond words, and went out of the forest of death back to the throne of royalty.

There king Śankara, standing as it were in the shoes of Amaraka, and indeed Amaraka himself as far as the eye could discern, learned all that pertained to the science and art of love, and so fitted himself to answer the probing questions of Sarasvatî. Meanwhile, however, the Ministers of State, finding their resuscitated râjan a far wiser and better man than ever before, suspected that there had been some such change of souls as we have described. They were loth to part with their new and wonderful king, so they issued a decree that the bodies of all those who had just passed on into the inner realms should be burnt. They hoped thereby that the mortal frame of this strange and beautiful being, now deserted, would be destroyed with the rest, and that thus he would remain a captive within the body of their king.

Time sped on, and Padmapada and the other devoted disciples, knowing not of the decree of the Ministers of State, left the body of their beloved master entrusted to their care, and journeyed towards the king's city. "Let us," said Padmapada, "appear before the king as singers, and weaving a message around our sweet music, let us tell him how we long for his return." It all came to pass as they had

planned; for as they stood before the supposed King Amaraka in the great hall of the palace, not only were those who
listened spellbound by their marvelous music, but its pellucid strains stole into the inner consciousness of Śankarâchârya. Before the bewildered attendants knew what had
befallen, Śankarâchârya gratefully dismissed the singers and
released himself from the corporeal chains that bound him.
His own body he found already upon the funeral pyre surrounded by angry flames that seemed to reach to the very
heavens. But it remained untouched by their destructive
power, and entering it, Śankara, shining with the illumination which streamed from his own being, descended from
the pyre and rejoined his devoted pupils, and together they
made their way to the house of Mandana Misra, who became a disciple of the young sage after hearing the last
question of Sarasvatî answered with keen wit and wisdom.

From this time on the beautiful messenger of the gods,
for such in truth he was, journeyed from city to city with
his faithful followers, spreading wherever he went his teachings of the Vedânta. It was indeed a spiritual and intellectual conquest. His words among the populace, in the
great cities or among the smaller towns and hamlets, in the
forests or along the highways, were like the falling of the
gentle rain after a season of drought and famine. His presence was like the glory of the morning sunlight when the
curtains of mist roll away from before the face of the sun.

Many are the stories told of his godlike powers, but were we
to recount these tonight, dawn would find us still gathered
here telling tales — tales of his bringing back to earth the
spirit of one departing, of his power to produce fire from the
palm of his right hand, of his ability to send his conscious-

ness whithersoever he willed. Those who are ignorant call these wonder-works miracles. Those who have knowledge of things behind this veil of illusion about us, know Śankara to be the greatest Initiate living in historical ages; and to the Initiate Nature makes obeisance, laying at his feet the key to her innermost secrets.

You have heard the words of one of the Wise Ones of the earth: "A few drops of rain do not make the monsoon, though they presage it." Thus does Śankarâchârya, unlike the ordinary mortal, perfected in wisdom, master of rare and occult powers, in appearance even like a god, stand as a prophecy of what we shall one day become in the far aeons of the future, yea, in that far distant time when the human host shall have made its long, long journey again and yet again through the seven spheres of its present home.

Until his thirty-second year this Sage of the East journeyed, carrying from land to land the blessing of his divine philosophy. Then his term of life was at an end, and into those heavenly realms where in joy the gods awaited him he disappeared in this wise: he absorbed his gross body into the subtil one and became existent; then destroying the subtil one into the body which is the cause of the world, he became pure intelligence; then attaining in the world of the Îśvara full happiness, unbroken, like a perfect circle, he became the intelligence which pervades the whole universe. Even now does he exist as the all-pervading intelligence. From above rang the grand paean of the gods echoing within the sacred places of the earth: "Victory!"

There is no higher coerse of joy
than silence where no mind pictur
dwells. p2

LaVergne, TN USA
28 April 2010
180889LV00004B/139/A